DRAMA SETS YOU FREE

A survey of the position of Drama in the curriculum
of secondary schools, undertaken by the
Secondary Heads Association 1998

MEMBERS OF THE WORKING PARTY

Peter Miller (Chair)
Wrenn School, Wellingborough

Robert Bray
Ilkeston School, Derby

Jean Gemmell
Fernwood Comprehensive School, Nottingham

Margaret Griffin (Vice President)
Axton Chase School, Kent

Philip Taylor
South Manchester High School

...

John Horn (Past President)
Analyst and Contributor

October 1998

CONTENTS

● PART 1

THE CURRENT POSITION OF DRAMA IN SECONDARY SCHOOLS

● PART 2

DRAMA IN SCHOOLS TODAY

● PART 3

STATISTICAL APPENDICES

● PART 4

EXTERNAL SUPPORT AGENCIES AND SCHOOL AND COLLEGE PRODUCTIONS 1996/1997

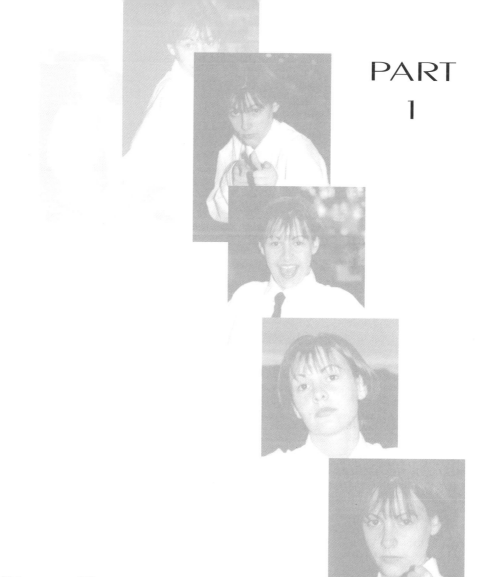

PART 1

THE CURRENT POSITION OF DRAMA IN SECONDARY SCHOOLS

THE QUESTIONNAIRE

This survey was designed to follow-up to the 1995 SHA enquiry which had resulted in the publication "**Whither the Arts?**" That report highlighted two particular issues for drama :

- *Should more value be put on drama in the curriculum?*

- *Is it regarded as 'amateur dramatics' rather than a major contributor to pupils' personal development ?*

Further, as drama is not treated as a separate subject within the National Curriculum, the questionnaire set out to discover :

Statistical information on :

- The organisation and staffing of drama in schools.

- The accommodation and facilities available.

- The availability of external support for the subject in schools.

- The teaching of drama in the KS3 curriculum.

- The courses, pupil numbers and examination successes in KS4.

- Syllabuses followed, and any particular reasons for their choice.

- Post - 16 drama provision (where appropriate).

- The wider use of drama techniques across the curriculum.

- Extra-curricular drama/theatre provision.

Views and comments on :

- Reasons for the increase, stability or decrease of drama in recent years.

- The benefits drama brings to pupils' personal and social development.

- The relationship between curricular and extra-curricular provision.

- Parental, governor and staff influence on the importance of drama in the school.

- The extent to which drama is perceived to be a vocational subject.

- The health, cost and benefits of school theatre productions, and staff involvement therein.

THE DATA-BASE

As identified in Appendix 1, 733 schools of various types responded to the President's invitation to take part in the survey. Please note :

- Where there were clear differences of interpretation on the precise information required, due notice has been taken in compiling the statistical analyses.

- Results are expressed as a percentage of schools who answered particular questions **not** the total sample.

- Statistics are mainly reported under the broad classification of mixed, boys' and girls' state (whether LEA, grant-maintained, comprehensive, grammar or secondary modern) and independent schools, though sometimes it seemed relevant to indicate grammar school responses separately.

- Attention is drawn in the text to where, within the broad classifications adopted, there is clear divergence from the general pattern.

- The request to indicate additional categories (Technology College etc.) and to give a brief analysis of intake, was to assist in achieving an appropriate balance when seeking possible case-studies.

THE RESPONDENTS

The Working Party is most grateful to all Heads, Deputies, Heads of Faculty or Department, and other staff who undertook the task of reply. Their roles are given in Appendix 2. Please note :

- Faculty Heads identified themselves under a wide range of titles including Creative Arts, Drama and Performing Arts, English and Drama, Expressive Arts, Performing Arts.

- Heads of Drama also used a variety of titles including Co-ordinator for Drama, Course Director for Drama, Curriculum Team Leader, Curriculum Manager, Head of Theatre Studies.

- Other contributors were English Teachers, Senior Teachers, Directors of Studies.

- In many cases where the Head had signed, clearly most of the response was supplied by a Head of Faculty or Department, but the Head (or sometimes a Deputy) had then completed Section VI, as requested, giving a personal, professional view on current trends.

THE FORMAT OF THE REPORT

The Working Party, fully aware that detailed statistical analyses, though useful as grounds for comparison for individual institutions, may not be the principal interest for readers, have adopted the following threefold approach to reporting the results in the next seven chapters:

- The principal findings.

- Commentary on issues and subsidiary findings.

- The Appendices. (See **Part Three.**)

Throughout the text italics are used where direct quotations from school responses are being used.

The members of the Working Party hope that this enquiry will provide a basis for debate and discussion within individual schools, the Branches, Regions and Council of SHA, and across the educational world, thus ensuring that the place of drama commands a higher profile in curriculum planning, as we judge this publication shows should be the case. Written responses will be welcomed as contributions to future debate. They should be sent to the Drama Working Party, Secondary Heads Association, 130 Regent Road, Leicester LE1 7PG.

PRINCIPAL FINDINGS

- Only half the schools have a specific separate independent drama department, and 15% have no such department at all.

- Nearly 25% of schools have no Head of Department for drama.

- Most Heads of Drama receive 1 or 2 promotion points.

- Drama departments are often not independently funded.

- Only 70% of staff teaching drama as a separate subject are qualified to do so, and the situation is worse where it is taught through the English curriculum.

- Curricular provision of drama is hampered by a lack of specialist accommodation in almost 50% of all schools. This results in frequent use of very unsuitable facilities.

ORGANISATION

Is there a separate drama department? (See Appendix 3)

Apart from respondents definitely reporting that they have , or have not, a separate drama department, interpretation of the statistics depends on understanding exactly how independent drama departments fit within a faculty structure. For some, drama is independent within a faculty; for others, it would be more fairly represented as a sub-set of the faculty, as when the post of 2 i/c English takes responsibility or the title Teacher i/c is used. Other trends to emerge included :

- Faculty structures are rare in independent and grammar schools, most frequent in mixed and girls' comprehensives.

- Boys' schools, and in particular boys' grammar schools, are the least likely to have a separate drama department.

- Almost exactly half (50.1%) of schools have a separate drama department, and a further 13% (noticeably girls' schools) identified a drama department within their Arts or English faculties.

- Though 15% of all schools said they have no separate department, 21% did confirm that drama was a specific part of a faculty or English department structure.

Heads of Drama and their remuneration. (See Appendix 4)

The introduction explains the wide variety of titles used by Heads of Drama, many also being designated Teacher i/c. In 23.2% of all schools there is no identified Head of Department, most commonly in LEA grammar schools. Some such postholders (8.3%) had other responsibilities, for example Head of Faculty, School Promotion or Community Arts - several schools stressed that drama was a key part of their community role. Sometimes a member of the school's Senior Management Team had oversight. With regard to remuneration the broad findings were :

- 2 or 1 promotion points are awarded most frequently.

- A greater number of points usually, but not always, indicates that other roles are undertaken.

- 10.9% of state and 30.6% of independent schools did not record the pay scale awarded. In the latter case this is probably because many independent schools have their own pay structure, which may also explain the higher percentage of such schools who specifically said there was no allowance.

- Sometimes the flexibility of awarding a half point is used, but there are also many examples of no financial recognition.

- Very rarely do schools award a point for a Second in Drama — seemingly when the Head of Department has other responsibilities.

- In independent schools points are sometimes tied to productions, with even a 4 points being awarded solely for extra-curricular drama.

How is drama funded?   (See Appendix 5)

In 25% of schools drama has no separate capitation, but of those 54.7% specifically allocate money through the English department or some faculty structure. It was again noticeable that only mixed comprehensives regularly use a faculty structure. Broadly the statistics are the same for state and independent schools, but it is worth noting :

- In both sectors single sex schools are less likely to have separate funding for drama.

- A minority of all schools depend wholly or partly on the revenue from productions.

- Independent schools occasionally charge special fees for tuition in drama.

● STAFFING QUALIFICATIONS (See Appendices 6 & 7)

A key indicator for the value given to drama in a school's curriculum is the extent to which those who teach it are fully qualified to do so. In the responses there were some variations in definition of "qualified". Some schools included as qualified those who may only have had a drama module in an English teaching qualification, others specified the difference between that and a full drama qualification. Due note has been taken of this and the broad picture given in the statistics and text accurately reflects the situation, as where there is no room for ambiguity - *" all teachers of English and Humanities are required to teach drama whether qualified or not "*

Appendix 6 gives the staffing details where drama (especially in KS3) is only taught through the English curriculum, Appendix 7 for where it is taught as an independent subject. In the latter, women outnumber men 2 to 1. They are in the majority in mixed (except independent) and even more in girls' schools, men in boys' schools. The pattern for qualifications is very similar in all schools, with 70% being qualified, but in particular it is worth noting :

- The highest proportion of qualified staff teach in single sex comprehensive and girls' independent schools.

- Strangely, girls' grammar schools are at the opposite end of the spectrum.

- Drama is not the main subject qualification for 43% of all staff teaching it in drama lessons (i.e. not those teaching it within English).

- Drama is taught through English in significantly more mixed and boys independent schools (39.6%) and all state grammar schools (50%), but only 18.5% of those English teachers are qualified to teach drama. Girls' independent schools are more in tune with the situation in state comprehensive and secondary modern schools.

- One school uses an interesting strategy to minimise any lack of specialism – a peripatetic drama specialist visits English groups in turn.

ACCOMMODATION (see Appendix 8)

Curriculum drama, as any other specialist subject, for effective delivery requires flexible specialist accommodation with appropriate equipment, lighting and other facilities. Comments like *"the needs of drama are not recognised by the time-tabling Deputy Head"* suggest that insufficient consideration is given to this issue in many schools - *"no specialist facilities for drama even in a brand new school in 1995"*. Elsewhere long-term deficiencies are recognised, with solutions being sought through achieving Arts status or, frequently, a successful lottery bid, usually in association with the local community.

Facilities in use

Appendix 8 gives an analysis of accommodation used by schools replying, in particular :

- Overall rooming for drama is very unsatisfactory in two respects.

    — Between 24 and 41% of schools have to use basic classrooms – it is difficult to communicate the importance of space – classrooms with tables around are dangerous.

    — 17.9% of curriculum drama takes place in spaces designed for other purposes, including dining rooms, gymnasia, huts, libraries, social areas, Youth Club and community facilities, even a chapel.

- Unsurprisingly between 40 and 51% of schools believe their delivery of drama is restricted by lack of specialist accommodation.

- Boys' schools, in particular grammar schools (where only 31% have drama rooms), have least specialist provision, yet even so feel least restricted.

- Girls' grammar schools are best provided with specialist drama rooms.

- Halls are used most frequently in single sex grammar and independent schools.

- 25% of independent schools have the benefit of designated theatres.

Commentary

Schools were invited to give more detailed views to supplement the raw statistics, from which the following emerged :

- Even schools with specialist accommodation suffer problems of disruption (*studio used for exams for 7/8 weeks*), lack of equipment, lighting and storage space.

- Use of halls brings many difficulties - constant interruptions, daily loss of time before and after dinner, breaks and assemblies, annual loss of space for examinations and school events, poor acoustics, everlasting negotiations with other subjects for shared use.

- Allocating a space is not enough – funds to refurbish must also be available.

- Restrictions on space too often limit student numbers, or prevent courses running – *it is hard to envisage drama beyond KS3 with no base – space is a very contentious issue.*

- Positively, some schools have invested heavily in improved facilities, often paid for by production profits and once by a generous donation from a retiring Head of Department's lump sum!

- Other schools strongly believe that drama is much more seriously restricted by lack of funds and/or appropriate staff than by poor accommodation – *the excellence of work shows that ideal accommodation is not as necessary as quality staff.*

- *Failure to recognise the value of drama in the National Curriculum makes it harder to justify specialist drama facilities in the light of deficit budgets* – excuse or hard fact?

● As one might expect **(see Appendix 9 and Part Four)**, this aspect of the survey reveals such differences of response from local authority, grant-maintained and independent schools respectively that overall statistics for all schools cannot give the true picture – differences in status determine the pattern of support available. Significant factors revealed in the statistics and explanatory comments included :

* Independent schools have least external support, though what they have is apparently less often charged for.

* Grant-maintained schools have virtually no free support.

* Only 29% of local authority schools report free help, and 12% specifically said their local authority provided nothing – *Nil from LEA – a total lack of importance given to the Arts by a culturally destitute and mean LEA.* The absence of such support is particularly damaging to single-handed departments.

* Advisers assist local authority schools most, but are bought in by nearly 20% of grant-maintained schools. However, county-wide advisers are rarely available as they have other conflicting subject responsibilities or, with the advent of new unitary authorities, are disappearing altogether.

* Grant-maintained schools particularly rely on local drama associations and personal networking.

* Theatre-in-Education groups are used uniformly across the state sector, but very rarely in independent schools which prefer other theatre groups. Both these agencies often assist with aspects of P.S.E., bullying, drugs, health education etc. (see a later chapter). T.I.E. is often described by schools as *wonderful but expensive.*

* To end on a cautionary note — all theatre groups *need careful choosing!*

PRINCIPAL FINDINGS

- Drama in KS3 is only compulsory, and taught as a separate subject, in 55% of schools.

- Attitudes to drama are significantly determined by the different types of school.

- Despite curricular pressure, drama is offered as a GCSE option in 80% of schools, most commonly in mixed comprehensives and secondary moderns.

- There still exist in some communities reservations about boys doing drama.

- Consistently, examination results in drama are better than in other subjects, but not because it is a soft option.

- Students deciding whether to choose drama at KS4 are more influenced by other factors than by whether the subject is available post-16.

KEY STAGE 3 (See Appendix 10)

The statistics show that nearly 75% of schools include drama as a compulsory element in the curriculum throughout KS3, but of those schools 27.6% only offer it within English. This does give rise to some concerns - see Appendix 6 on the qualifications of those teaching drama through English.

- *If drama is delivered in KS3 English there is considerable variation according to the teacher.*

- *The use of non-specialist drama/English teachers reduces the number and effectiveness of drama lessons in KS3.*

- *I am very worried about the slide away from separate subject to English department – their specialist staff are not trained to deliver drama and tend to regard it as "doing plays".*

In the remaining 25% of schools, provision of drama is restricted. It is either not available at all, or only in some year groups or for some pupils. Direct quotations reveal very different perceptions on the relative importance of drama in the curriculum.

- *Drama is compulsory in KS3 except for double linguists.*

- *KS3 has a circus of Drama, Rural Science and Study Skills for the lower half of the year.*

- *The Curriculum Development Group nearly recommended drama for all, but it was squashed by "trad" HODs.*

- *Ofsted 1997 suggested drama for all to improve oral skills.*

- *The curriculum is deficient for lack of drama, but short of time, staff and accommodation.*

- *Drama is very important in a boys only school, but has less curricular provision than Art or Music.*

When drama is available it is taught as a separate subject in 55% of schools, in 15% through a variety of Arts or other circuses, in 30% delivered via English.

Appendix 10 also points up the variation, sometimes significant, in the attitude to drama between different types of school, comprehensives and secondary moderns, grammar and independent, mixed, boys and girls. Most relevant seem to be :

- Drama appears as a compulsory subject least frequently in independent and grammar schools — only girls' independent and mixed grammar schools buck this trend (for interest, note the Case Study, Wilmington G.S.).

- There is a marked preference in grammar schools to deliver drama through English, and Arts circuses are very rare.

- Comprehensive and secondary modern schools are most committed to compulsory drama and to teaching it as a separate subject.

- In boys' comprehensives, as in all other boys' schools, drama is more regularly part of the English curriculum.

Such differences of emphasis between schools on the importance of drama within the curriculum, and the quotations above, highlight the plea, often repeated throughout the survey :

Drama should be in the National Curriculum!

It is a travesty that drama does not have its own status in the National Curriculum. To see it as "part of English" is to fail to recognise its all-embracing significance.

KEY STAGE 4 (See Appendix 11)

Drama, in common with many other subjects, suffers considerable curriculum squeeze in KS4 Option Schemes. Particular difficulties are revealed in comments like :

- *National Curriculum constraints make drama compete with a wide range of subjects.*

- *Drama suffered when compulsory Technology and Modern Foreign Language were introduced.*

- *If able girls choose drama they miss out on 2nd Foreign Language/Humanities.*

- *In a small boys' comprehensive there is the will to offer drama, but this would mean displacing subject.*

- *In a girls' independent school, given the range of subjects at KS4, the inclusion of an extra one was not especially desirable.*

In the circumstances it is pleasing to report that 80% of all schools offer drama. though Appendix 11 reveals significant differences in practice. Most relevantly :

- Drama features as a GCSE option in the vast majority of comprehensive and secondary modern, but only half grammar and independent schools.

- Mixed schools are most likely to offer the subject, boys' the least.

- Combined courses occur very rarely, usually in mixed schools and girls' comprehensives, and not at all in grammar schools.

- In 25% of grammar schools pupils have to do some drama in KS4. specifically within English, 20% of other girls' schools follow the same pattern, other boys' schools never.

Combined courses and a strong belief in a compulsory Creative Arts subject at KS4, can both support drama in the curriculum – *Drama should be part of the Arts entitlement at KS4.* Some schools offset timetabling pressure by offering drama off-timetable, after school. Another interesting strategy was – *in KS4 all do Art, Music or Drama in 2 periods, and can convert to an examination course in an extra two periods.*

Gender balance in mixed schools (see Appendix 12)

The raw statistics showed approximately half the schools having some gender imbalance. However, more interesting is the analysis of comments made. There are four principal factors :

- **The gender of teachers** – apparently works both ways.

  — *Generally pupils tend to be the same sex as the drama teacher.*

  — *Male staff are needed to encourage boys.*

  — *Other male staff put boys off drama.*

- **The structure of option choice** — Boys are in the majority if drama is only available for lower ability groups, girls, if it is set against Sports Studies. Even choices made in KS3 *upset the balance in year 7 where pupils are required to opt in years 8/9 for drama against second foreign language, information technology etc.*

- **Syllabus content** — *we are trying to correct gender imbalance by introducing more technical skills.*

- **Local culture** — influencing boys against choosing drama is very hard to counteract, despite one reported success – *boys' numbers are improving, with an enhanced perception of the subject by staff and parents.* Even within a school prejudices may exist – *boys are heavily advised against drama – sexism!,* though more commonly the problem is more widespread :

- *Still trying to counter sub-cultural stereotyping.*

- *Very difficult to undermine the inherent machismo of a mining community.*

GCSE syllabuses

Schools were asked to identify the GCSE Syllabuses they are using, and why they had been chosen. The latter question was rather easier to analyse, so varied were the responses to the first, with some respondents only identifying a syllabus by number, some by title, some by alternative papers within a syllabus, others using outdated titles both for examinations and Boards. After valuable assistance from Helen Weatherson, Examination and Assessment Officer at Wrenn School, to whom many thanks, it seemed best to confirm that there were at the time four main providers, EDEXCEL, MEG, NEAB and SEG, and then to analyse why individual schools chose them. This might assist schools in any future review of their choice of syllabus, which might be necessitated by the recent re-organisation of Examination Boards into AQA, EDEXCEL and OCR.

The statistical pattern of choice, SEG 31.4%, EDEXCEL 27%, MEG 21%, NEAB 20.6% was very similar throughout all schools, though it was noticeable that grammar and independent schools showed a marked preference for SEG and MEG in that order. Four other Boards were occasionally mentioned, AEB in England and, for obvious geographical and cultural reasons, NICCEA, SEB and WJEC.

Why are particular syllabuses chosen?

1. Reasons not specific to a syllabus

- Personal choice by teachers – most commonly because a teacher is also an examiner for a Board, and thus has a voice in syllabus development for the subject.

- School policy – some schools ordain that all subjects use the same Board.

2. Reasons common to all Boards

- Good support for individual departments with Boards providing Inset and encouraging networking among their schools, sometimes by consortia.

- A strong practical element with an emphasis on improvisation and performance with the flexibility to use other skills.

3. Particular strengths attributed to Boards (sometimes the same, though couched in different terms)

EDEXCEL

- Student-centred philosophy.

- Natural progression from KS3.

- Good balance between practice and theory, offering scope for students of every ability to succeed.

- Excellent assessment programme through internal/external moderation, with no formal written examination.

- Sound basis for Theatre Studies.

MEG

- Best philosophy, offering variety, freedom and flexibility.

- Appropriate for the full range of ability, designed to stretch every pupil.

- Issues based, encouraging social/thinking skills, creative decision-making and responsibility.

- One has written examination; the other two have an exam, one text-based and the other stimulus-based. Both use pre-release material.

- Good basis for Theatre Studies.

NEA

- Natural progression from KS3.

- Range of options including practical elements like stagecraft.

- Excellent balance in continuous assessment procedures, sensibly moderated.

SEG

- Suitable for mixed ability teaching, with group culture able to improve results, but by no means a soft option.

- Rigorous and a good academic preparation for A Level – *a structured syllabus, stretching the able and the best introduction for future A Level.*

- Good range of options **BUT** considerable alarm at recent changes in syllabus, particularly the introduction of written work – some schools have already changed Boards for this reason.

The quality of examination results in drama

Schools were asked to indicate how their examination results in drama compared with those for other subjects, difficult to answer in view of so many variables. Nonetheless both statistics and comments provided by 485 schools suggest that drama regularly brings success to pupils of all abilities. Combining responses such as – *compares well* or – *very favourably* with results are – *good, – excellent, – consistently better, – best* or – *above average* we have 83.3%. A further 12.4% (notably mixed and girls' independent schools) felt they were – *similar* or – *the average expected*, while only 4.3% reported results as – *below average* or *poor*.

Explanatory comments sometimes seemed defensive, fearful that drama might be regarded a soft option. True, in some schools the subject is more often chosen by lower ability pupils, but for them enthusiasm and commitment to a subject they enjoy often bring greater success in drama than elsewhere, suggesting higher motivation rather than an intrinsically easier option. Direct quotations included :

- *Results are good (absolutely), not because easier.*

- *Poor results are caused by a lack of commitment to the course work element.*

- *Some students achieve success at drama but little else.*

- *Results are above average for both school and students.*

- *Results compare very favourably for all abilities.*

PROVISION FOR DRAMA POST-16 (See Appendix 13)

The statistics need careful interpretation, noting in particular the size of samples. Almost all grammar and independent schools replied because they have Sixth Forms, many comprehensives and secondary moderns do not. However, some such schools reported where Drama/Theatre Studies is available elsewhere for their students post-16. Also included as affirmative replies are schools who have courses other than A Level in years 12 & 13, and provision in consortia.

All types of school gave broadly similar answers to both the questions asked. Post - 16 drama courses are least available in grammar and boys' schools. Understandably, for the same group curriculum choice at KS4 is least affected, though girls' schools reflect the same view. Very different attitudes to post -16 provision are shown by the following comments, principally from independent schools :

- *Theatre Studies is in its first year – already a significant positive impact on the self – confidence of students and the schools as a whole.*

- *There is parental prejudice about acceptability.*

- *No drama in Post-16 curriculum – it would distort A Level choice in an academic school.*

- *The take-up is small, concern regarding acceptability to Universities – would like to counter.*

- *More relevant is the size of Sixth Form – if small you cannot afford A Level Theatre Studies*

- *We stress extra-curricular drama, and offer an option in General Studies.*

A smaller sample of schools were prepared to commit themselves on whether the availability of drama post-16 influences curriculum choice at KS4. Many of those replying in the negative gave alternative, more relevant, factors, and some positively asserted that the opposite was true :

- *The enthusiasm of staff is the major factor,*

- *The reputation of results at GCSE and delivery at KS3 (is it well taught and enjoyable?) are more influential.*

- *The presence of A level does give academic respectability.*

- *In Scotland there is the requirement for a creative/aesthetic subject in years 3/4.*

- *Many choosing drama are not suitable for academic courses.*

- *Drama at GCSE is popular, enjoyable, developing confidence and communication skills.*

- *Extra-curricular productions pre-16 encourage Theatre Studies post-16.*

- *We intend to use GNVQ provision to build on drama at KS4.*

PRINCIPAL FINDINGS

- Extra-curricular drama is flourishing in most schools.

- While the majority firmly believe there is a positive valuable relationship between curricular and extra-curricular drama, a minority equally strongly believe they should be regarded as distinct.

Extra-curricular drama is alive and kicking in the vast majority of schools – only 5.7% replied that they had little or no such activity. The variety recorded is impressive, though it is sometimes unclear whether different schools are describing the same activity in different terms. For all schools therefore the results are presented as numbers rather than percentages, because rarely were clear differences of pattern of provision discernible, except that most commonly in the year :

- Girls' comprehensives and mixed grammar schools had just one major production.

- Independent schools had several major productions.

- Mixed comprehensives took drama to primary schools.

- Drama Clubs featured in girls' schools.

- Independent schools staged House/Form drama competitions.

ACTIVITIES RECORDED FOR 1996/97 (NUMBER OF SCHOOLS REPORTING IN BRACKETS)

One major production in the year (277). See Appendix 17 and Part Four.

More than one major production in the year (169)

Presentations, showcase or studio performances by GCSE/A Level students (208)

Drama Clubs/Theatre Groups, variously described, for one or more Year-Groups, Lower/Middle School, lunchtime, after school etc (397). Such activities are often organised by older for younger students.

Form and Year Group productions (95)

House or Form Drama Competitions (54)

Drama to Primary Schools (52)

Arts and Drama Festivals (44)

Other activities (119) including Activities Weeks, Cabaret Evenings, Charity Evenings, Christmas productions, Community Arts Theatre/Groups, Concerts, Drama Weekends, Foreign Links, Impromptu Performances, National Competitions, Pantomimes, Performances for Senior Citizens, School Events, Talent Shows, Variety Nights, Writers Groups.

Very little or none (42)

IS THERE AN INTERRELATIONSHIP BETWEEN CURRICULAR AND EXTRA-CURRICULAR PROVISION FOR DRAMA?

Affirmative answers to this question were nearly 90%, though the connection was less clearly supported by boys' independent and all grammar schools. Much more interesting were the wide variety of perspectives on the nature of the relationship, and the powerful denials of the minority. A number of issues commanded wide support :

- Curricular and extra-curricular drama have different qualities, often different participants, aims and purposes, but interrelated skills. They feed each other, but are not necessarily formally linked.

- *I agree with Heathcote et al that the difference is a matter of degree not kind. All drama is metaphor, and a means of exploring / illuminating life.*

- On the choice of productions :

There is potentially a tension – "straight" drama is under pressure from big musicals, and "straight" drama is likely to give preference to examination candidates in drama, to the detriment of others.

The Theatre Studies group give a professional edge, but can inhibit choice of production to the "serious".

- Neither aspect should invade the other's time :

Curriculum drama, if demanding extra-curricular rehearsal time, can invade other extra-curricular provision.

I can't emphasise the connection enough – but productions rehearsed entirely after school, and lessons are independent of extra-curricular work.

The influence of extra-curricular activities on curricular provision, both in general and for individual students, generated widely disparate views. For some they compensated for the lack of GCSE or for students who had to make other subject choices :

- *Make them keen by class drama in KS3, then concentrate on extra-curricular (a deliberate decision not to offer GCSE).*

- *Extra-curricular is the only way drama can be extended beyond Year 8.*

- *They fill the gap for those who are not able, or who prefer, to choose other subjects within the option scheme.*

- *Props up the lack of curriculum time.*

For others, extra-curricular activities positively promote curriculum drama:

- *The high standard of extra-curricular activities promoted GCSE.*

- *If there is little access to drama beyond Year 7, students are less willing to be involved in productions.*

- *Pupils in school productions are more likely to opt for GCSE.*

- *Assists the balance between boys and girls at KS4.*

However, as previously identified, a minority strongly felt there neither is nor should be an interrelationship. Rather they are separate entities. Curriculum drama is educational drama, a subject in its own right, with aims, objectives and a syllabus. It is not designed simply to develop techniques for extra-curricular work. Direct quotations explain best :

- *I tend to see them as separate issues. Curriculum drama is concerned with particular themes relevant to each year group in KS3. Extra-curricular is more concerned with excellence in performance.*

- *Drama in the curriculum should be noted for educational merits, as distinct from its extra-curricular benefits.*

- *Builds on relationships founded in the classroom, but I refuse to imply or create expectation for involvement in voluntary activities.*

- *Instead of extending drama students, extra-curricular drama gets turned into a PR exercise, losing its educational value in the process.*

- *Drama has a major educational role – not geared to productions.*

- *Drama does need to be valued as an art form in its own right – drama as drama, not as theatre.*

There was massive evidence for the view that there is an essential positive interrelationship. Curriculum drama, often through staff commitment and excellent teaching, generates and maintains enthusiasm. Extra-curricular drama raises the profile and status of drama, provides a focus to develop work beyond the classroom and extends student perception of drama. Quality in either enhances and complements the other; they cannot be separated. Particular comments (some cautionary!) included:

- *Extra-curricular the shop window, curriculum the store room.*

- *I try to teach skills necessary for extra-curricular drama in the classroom, as well as developing imagination and oral, teamwork and confidence skills.*

- *Curriculum drama supplies kudos, enthusiasm and developing expertise for extra-curricular activities – commitment there feeds back positively into the classroom.*

- *I prefer that much of what is seen publicly **closely** reflects what goes on in the classroom.*

- *Extra-curricular drama allows practised skills to be demonstrated, it raises the profile in parents' eyes, **but** a double-edged sword when some parents see drama as "acting".*

- *It is sometimes necessary to dispel the "stagey" amateur dramatics view of drama.*

- *A level of curricular provision is an essential basis for any performance activity and relates to the acquisition of skills, discipline and standards of the actors.*

- *To work without exhibiting or performing is simply a waste of time.*

- *It reinforces and stimulates interest, involvement and relevance. It helps to maintain the positive "can I take it home to show my parents" so obvious in KS 1 & 2 but not in 3 & 4.*

- *Drama is meant for audience.*

PRINCIPAL FINDINGS

- Drama contributes far beyond its own curriculum area in most schools.

- The type and extent of use depends most on the personality and enthusiasm of individual teachers.

- Personal and social education, assemblies, and other subjects using role play, benefit most.

- All schools identify confidence, communication skills, teamwork and understanding as the four most important benefits.

- Drama clearly contributes comprehensively to personal and social development.

WIDER USES (See Appendix 14)

Drama permeates our lives here - not all felt so strongly but undoubtedly for the majority of schools Drama provides far more than just its own contribution to the timetabled curriculum. Only a tiny minority of schools either did not reply or specifically said that drama was not used elsewhere. Most schools reported either their use of drama techniques like role-play (hot seating, freeze frames and thought-tapping were also mentioned) or drama's regular input to Personal and Social Education and Assemblies. Drama also supports other subjects within the curriculum, school events and in-service training.

The pattern revealed is remarkably similar for all schools, probably because the extent to which drama is used depends less upon the type of school (mixed, boys', girls', grammar, independent than upon the talent and interest of individual teachers. The comment *wider use depends upon the confidence of teachers* was confirmed by evidence that staff other than drama specialists are often nervous about using drama, fearing some loss of control. Staff also feel concern about the contrasting atmosphere in lessons using drama and those requiring a more orderly environment – *Drama can have a destabilising effect*. Drama teachers expressed reservations about the wider use of role-play – *sometimes a dangerous practice when delivered by non-specialist drama staff.* Such difficulties can be, and clearly often are, overcome where Theatre in Education and other groups are available to come in especially for P.S.E., but as shown in a previous chapter such provision is distinctly patchy. Despite such reservations it is worth noting:

- Role-play is used significantly less in boys' comprehensive and grammar schools.

- The use of drama in P.S.E. is least frequent in girls' grammar and boys' comprehensive schools.

- Use in Assemblies occurs much more often in mixed independent, all grammar and all girls' schools.

Assemblies

It is common practice to ask Form-Tutors and their Forms to take responsibility for Assemblies on a regular or occasional basis. Most often a group of students give a drama presentation, usually on an issue such as one of those outlined in the next paragraph. The confidence and extrovert nature required for such assemblies may explain the finding above on where it happens most frequently. Reservations were also expressed – *as Head of Department I worry about bad drama organised by non-specialists for entertainment value in assemblies - it does not promote the subject, rather it damages it.*

Personal And Social Education

The statistics confirm how widespread is the use of drama in this curriculum area. Careers (role-play for individual interviews and business management scenarios on Industry Days) and Health are commonly included, sometimes added to the title. So inter-related are the topics recorded that it seems most helpful to list, under broad headings, all aspects of PSE where drama is used to emphasise the issues. Suffice to say that bullying, drugs, road-safety and sex education were mentioned most.

- Drugs – including alcohol and smoking.

- Environmental and social – gender and equal opportunities, litter, prejudice, racism, road-safety, school and community action.

- Health and Sex Education – abortion, aids and anorexia.

- Law and Order – crime prevention, domestic violence, joy-riding, shoplifting, youth crime.

- Relationships – bullying, peer pressure.

Drama In Other Subjects

The views that – *drama has great potential as a cross-curricular medium,* and – *drama is a teaching strategy* are fully confirmed by an analysis of all the subjects to which drama contributes. Significantly an Arts College says *all*. Nearly 34% of all schools mentioned some aspect of English (or Welsh), including debates and public-speaking. Other subjects that figured prominently were History/Humanities (27.5%), Modern and Classical Languages (17%) and Religious Education (12.4%). Perhaps more surprising is the frequency with which Geography and Science use drama, and that every subject was mentioned occasionally.

School Events

The important contribution of drama to school life is not restricted to the curriculum. An earlier chapter details the range of specialist extra-curricular activities provided, but under this heading of "wider uses" schools listed a variety of official school events in which drama plays a part, including:

Community Service, Fund-raising, Open Evenings, Parents' Evenings, Promoting the School, Pupil Induction, Residential Weeks, Theme Weeks.

Support For Staff

Finally, and importantly in light of comments above on the key role of teachers, schools recorded the use of drama for In-Service Training. It is regarded as valuable for training and supporting teachers in their role as counsellors. Not least, one Senior Management Team emphasised its value to themselves.

BENEFITS

No time to answer was an understandable response — the list of benefits identified is so long that analysis and summary proved difficult. It seems best therefore to provide a short summary, then identify in greater detail the wide-ranging vocabulary used, sometimes supported by quotations, and finally to allow respondents' words to speak for themselves.

Summary

Detailed consideration of responses from all types of school, apart from the 8.5% who were content to reply briefly, but positively, *enormous, immense, massive,* reveals unanimity. The benefit mentioned most is always confidence, the next three, though not always in the same order, communication skills, teamwork and understanding. Listed below, under broad headings, is the variety of words used by respondents to describe the multiple benefits that they believe drama brings.

Communication skills — language development, listening, negotiating, oracy, rote-learning, self-expression.

Through its promotion of oracy, drama has the potential to make a significant contribution to the improvement of literacy.

Inter-personal qualities and skills — consideration, co-operation, relationships, respect, socialisation, teamwork, tolerance, trust.

The world's greatest team game.

Issues — equal opportunities, moral/social, personal.

Provides an opportunity to explore issues without the block of writing/reading that some students experience.

Outcomes — citizenship, enjoyment and understanding of theatre, exhilaration of participation, positive attitude to/ experience of school, relaxation, school ethos.

Drama is an essential component in the cultural life of the school.

Personal development — emotional, maturity, personal ownership, physical, social.

Very important for boys in dealing with feelings.

It's a whole philosophy of the benefits of the aesthetic to the development of spiritual values.

Personal qualities — assertiveness (girls), concentration, confidence, creativity, enthusiasm, imagination, independence, initiative, leadership, pride, reflectiveness (boys), reliability, responsibility, self-discipline, self esteem, sensitivity.

Personal skills — analysis, awareness/empathy/understanding (body language, cultural insight, media pressure, other people's eyes, peers, self), decision-making, managing disability, problem-solving, risk-taking.

Gives boys strong opportunities to develop affective skills and vocabulary.

Process — in role, not teacher dominated, safe exploration of ideas, success (not available elsewhere).

Drama is excellent for giving a sense of self-worth to many children who may be failures in our traditional academic subjects.

Opportunity to shine.

Enormous benefits enabling pre-experience of problems in a safe controlled environment.

Where do I start?! I have seen, over 12 years, so many pupils develop in so many ways through doing drama – not so much in the "performance" elements, but in the process which it puts them through. Group co-operation, problem-solving, self discipline, creativity. potential for empathy, sensitivity, confidence, versatility, communication skills .... I would go so far as to say that it is vital to a lot of pupils' development.

Drama is an extension of "child's play" which offers students the chance to work through an "imagined world" in order to understand, through the protective fiction, themselves and the world they live in. Students are encouraged to see themselves as decision makers and problem solvers who can operate collaboratively to explore not only a range of human feelings but also a whole spectrum of social, moral, ethical and spiritual dilemmas.

Quotations

Direct quotations are grouped in three sections. First there are those which give a comprehensive explanation of the contribution of drama to the personal and social development of pupils.

Drama is vital for a pupil's personal and social development and should be compulsory in all schools at least until the end of KS3.

Enhancing skills of Concentration, Communication, Co-operation, Co-ordination, Control, Confidence and Creativity (I call it the 7 Cs).

Drama is a catalyst. All children eventually grow and mature but drama often speeds up the process especially in areas of emotion, aesthetic appreciation, self confidence etc. To be a doctor it is appropriate to take science subjects; an accountant would have a maths background, but where do the everyday skills needed to succeed in any job come from i.e. communication, interpersonal, listening, organisational and problem-solving skills? Drama can cover all of these. A question I ask of pupils "Do you want to be involved in I.T. or do you want to be in charge of those involved in I.T.?

Incalculably beneficial. It enhances pupils' self-belief. It encourages and nurtures the basic skills of co-operation, commitment and control. It allows and encourages pupils to see "through others' eyes" and develops their empathetic understanding. It has the power to explore, shape and change feelings and ideas.

The main value of drama is perhaps the development of confidence and in pupils' oral interaction in lessons. Pupils are encouraged to reflect on their interpretation of their experiences; it empowers understanding and encourages the development of value systems that can inform behaviour. It is an essential part of personal development.

Drama builds self esteem by harnessing the pleasure all children have in "play" in its widest sense and allowing them to shape and explore their own experience by working in role. Working in role and creating a character provides a space that is both safe and yet full of possibility. Writing in role is all the more powerful because it is experienced. We notice that our pupils have poise and confidence in front of audiences; are better able to empathise with the feelings of others; can manage relationships with peers and adults sensitively; have pride in the quality of their performance work and acquire cultural knowledge.

Confidence, identity, understanding of wider issues of gender, race. equality, history, cultures, tolerance. There is a therapeutic element to the subject which helps young people deal with the demands of growing up as part of the community and world as a whole.

Drama encourages all pupils to be confident contributors. It allows them to explore issues and concerns in an imaginative and thought- provoking way. It can lead to a deepening of understanding of their own lives and the world about them. It develops self-discipline, respect for themselves and tolerance for others.

Drama is P.S.E.!! *It has been re-named, re-packaged and generally speaking is delivered badly by teachers who are not specialists. What else should we expect? Drama is a process, as is the development of the child. It is metaphoric and analytic. Drama conventions can be employed to highlight situations differently. Drama releases children so they are free to develop their own ideas and reach their own conclusions. They draw on their personal observations of life to develop and resolve the situation their own way using natural speech and movement. They have the opportunity to elucidate their ideas by sincerely expressing them without being inhibited or limited by technique. By this process wider channels of communication are opened. Vague impressions are brought into sharp focus, puzzling impressions are re-understood, fragmentary ones are completed and alarming ones are faced. Imaginative observation is stimulated and our understanding of ourselves and our environment is extended and deepened.*

Drama has a unique contribution to the education of children; social drama, expression, control, engagement with the inner self are all vital.

Some schools see a specific benefit of drama in that it provides necessary balance in the curriculum.

It counteracts the pressures of a school that places an overemphasis on achievement.

Breaks up a fairly academic National Curriculum for pupils whose concentration is not total.

For many of our girls it is both a welcome relief from more formal lessons and an excellent means of expressing difficult ideas and feelings.

Finally there are some who do not teach drama for the personal and social development of pupils, but nonetheless recognise the benefits it brings.

I do not see drama as a service industry and do not justify my subject in terms of social education. It is an art form in its own right. But incidental benefits are manifold; using drama to explore issues thus enhancing understanding of humanity; sensitivity towards others and their work; communication is at the core of drama and I can think of no more important life skill; confidence – to name but four.

We teach drama as a subject with its own body of knowledge, skills and disciplines, not as an area which is deliberately therapeutic for pupils. However, the use of group work, concentration on the body for communication and some of the issues addressed in lessons inevitably contributes towards the pupils' social and personal development – it is inevitable.

This chapter reflects the personal informed opinions of the leaders of the schools who responded to the survey, though it is also important to emphasise that they are often reporting their perception on what other staff in the school think, not necessarily their own view.

PRINCIPAL FINDINGS

- Provision for drama has increased in more than 50% of schools.

- The vision and leadership of the Headteacher and/or the Head of Department is the most important factor for increase.

- Omission from the National Curriculum is the principal reason for decrease, and for stability where it prevents expansion.

- A significant majority of schools, especially independent, expect an increase for drama in the next few years.

- Parents and governors can, and do, often positively influence decisions on drama.

- Staff of all subject disciplines also influence the priority given to drama in the curriculum, both as individuals and collectively.

- Drama is rarely perceived as vocational except in the sense that it encourages qualities valuable in any specific vocation.

- Despite numerous costs and difficulties productions are healthy in 75% of schools.

- Not least among the benefits from school productions is developing an understanding of what it means to be part of an audience.

- The principal motivation for many staff involved in productions is to help students achieve success.

HAS DRAMA INCREASED, REMAINED STABLE OR DECREASED? (See Appendix 15)

Whilst it is encouraging that drama is on the increase in over 50% of all schools, it is a cause for concern that drama has decreased in about 11%. Specifically :

- Schools of all genders had very similar patterns of increase, but boys' schools reported significantly more, girls' schools notably less decrease.

- The positive trend for drama is remarkably consistent in grammar and independent schools.

- Decrease was greatest in boys' grammar schools, but not reported at all in mixed grammar and girls' independent schools.

Many schools gave reasons for increase (392), stability (18) or decrease (94). Though many answers were predictable, nonetheless the primary influence of the vision and leadership from Headteachers, Heads of Department and other staff is well worth emphasising. Reasons given for **an increase**, under broad headings, are (the number of comments is in the bracket) :

- Departmental factors — the quality of teaching by all staff (often shown by excellent examination results – *success breeds success*) and, in particular, the enthusiasm and charisma of Heads of Department. Specifically there were 55 comments on the impetus derived from new appointments and additional specialists (197).

- Curricular factors, including revised structures for option choice following review, new policies on curriculum balance (*Arts for all*), reaction to Ofsted, the introduction of GCSE or syllabus changes within it. *The National Curriculum reduced the status - we raised it!*

- Pupils — their own enthusiasm, fuelled by positive experiences in KS3 and extra-curricular activities, creates demand, more frequently supported now by parental awareness of the value of drama (54).

- Headteachers, variously described as *passionate*, *visionary, innovative,* often newly appointed – their influence, frequently associated with the Senior Management Team and Governors, is often critical for drama' s priority in a school. The survey rarely found any need to draw attention to grant-maintained status, but here *"Grant-maintained status allows us to decide our own priorities".* (47).

- New accommodation and facilities (18).

- An interesting duo – the advent of girls in the Sixth Form, and as a recruiting tactic.

Only 18 replies gave detailed reasons for **stability**, but all had a common factor – expansion was desirable, but prevented by lack of staff, funds or accommodation, and above all by National

Curriculum pressure on KS 3 & 4. A determined effort is needed to overcome such concerns :

- *The school's aims defended drama against National Curriculum squeeze.*

- *A few ups and downs in our provision – now back to full strength, but we always tend to feel the most vulnerable area of school and have to work hard to justify our existence.*

The overwhelming reason for **decrease** is curricular – the subject's absence from the National Curriculum. One comment gives cause for alarm - *Drama is a victim of the Woodhead agenda.* To which might be added League Tables because many schools and staff feel they must concentrate on the basics, to the neglect of subjects perceived to be peripheral. Reasons given in detail were :

- Curricular factors – not in the National Curriculum, reduced option choice with compulsory Technology / Modern Foreign Language, crowded out in K.S.3 by I.T. and P.S.E. (though see elsewhere for the benefits drama brings to P.S.E.), changes in GCSE syllabus (52).

- Staffing factors – loss of specialists, reduction in staff, even staff attitudes. The influence of a curriculum Deputy Head, believing drama only for the non-academic, can disadvantage the subject. (24).

- Lack of facilities and funding – (11).

- Also referred to were student choice and lack of extra-curricular activity.

WHAT DEVELOPMENTS ARE EXPECTED?

Responses on the future often replicated those for the past – the relevant factors (curriculum, staff, funding) are the same.

Neutrally, some accepted – *it depends upon the government.* In schools which anticipated less drama the principal concerns were possible effects from cuts in staffing, reduced funding and curricular pressure and the subject's lack of status in the National Curriculum. Detailed worries included submersion into English and changes in syllabus and fear that curricular autonomy might be lost. Specific views:

- *National targets delivery could reduce time.*

- *As a discrete subject it requires too big a chunk of time-table time.*

- *Concern if grant-maintained status and autonomy disappear.*

- *Without support at national level many Heads (especially those without Arts backgrounds) are likely to see drama as an easy target for cost-cutting.*

However, positive comments outnumbered reservations 2 to 1, with independent schools notably totally positive. Reasons given are the precise reverse of concerns expressed. Some schools expect new staff to make a difference, others to have improved accommodation and extra resources, sometimes associated with current bids for Lottery Funds or Arts or Magnet College status. Curriculum expansion was expected at all Key Stages - to be disentangled from English in all or part of 3, GCSE introduced in 4 and a variety of post-16 courses in 5. Parental pressure was mentioned, as were governors and a revitalised extra-curricular programme. Quotations included :

- We want drama to be more central to the education of girls.

- Drama to become integral to every child's curriculum.

THE VIEWS OF PARENTS AND GOVERNORS (SEE APPENDIX 16)

Whether or not parents or governors formally influence decisions on drama, the value of their support and active encouragement, or lack of it (*parents' unwillingness to attend productions disheartens staff*), was constantly emphasised, particularly for extra-curricular productions. Interpretation of statistics is difficult - parental and governor views seem to count most in grammar schools, parental views least in comprehensive, governors' least in independent schools. Statistics apart, comments prove how often both groups play a significant role.

For parents there is less formal opportunity, but firm views are often put. *Some parents complain about compulsory Arts in Key Stage 4.* In contrast, other parents, jointly with their offspring, petitioned the governors for GCSE drama, and in one school *"I succumbed to parental pressure to teach drama"*. There was one very sad comment, hopefully rare, *"We are not important - we are useful for school plays etc. but nothing else"*.

Governors' decisions often affect drama in school. Some are doubters:

- *A few wish to see more academic subjects.*

- *A few come to productions but on the whole don't understand the potential of drama.*

Many more are proactive in support and keen to expand drama:

- *Governors regard this as essential.*

- *Drama is increasingly seen as a high status subject.*

- *Not directly but school ethos values creative activity.*

Support is variously shown - formal approval of the curriculum, plans for improved accommodation, staff appointment strategy, either for a new post as Head of Department or, critically – *in a redundancy situation, stipulated drama to remain separate and unchanged.*

THE INFLUENCE OF STAFF

What influence have members of staff **(whatever their subject discipline)** on the provision of drama? In 715 responses a very similar pattern emerged in all types of school, though independent, and to a lesser extent grammar, schools appeared to have extra-curricular drama more in mind when replying. Significantly 75% of all comments were positive in tone, with 20% negative and the rest neutral.

The neutral group did confirm the crucial importance of staff attitudes towards drama, though some would just leave it to the English department. Opinions are divided in lively debate – what is drama's true educational worth? What priority should it have?

- *Those interested in personal development convinced that drama is an essential element in the curriculum – many unconvinced.*

- *Some supportive, corporate loyalty to any school activity – some adverse reaction to conflicts of time and priority.*

- *Importance recognised but not perceived as a priority.*

- *Most support but still seen as an 'easy option', not a priority.*

- *Drama would take over the school if not controlled.*

70% of negative answers simply stated that other staff had little or no influence. More particular concerns centred on relations with the English department, and /or other Heads of Department, the intrusive nature of productions and a perceived lack of understanding of the role of drama. Views on the first were ambivalent, with the English department either insufficiently supportive, not seeing drama as a priority, or wishing to retain it fully themselves - *there is an ingrained resistance to drama moving outside the English department.* In the context of a crowded curriculum at KS3 and 4 the negative pressure of other Heads of Departments may seem understandable:

- *Faculties wanting more time in Year 9 see drama as a non-National Curriculum luxury.*

- *Some Heads of Department see it as a threat, especially in the option scheme - they are jealous of KS4 take-up.*

Understandable too are tensions aroused by productions (*the release of pupils for rehearsals creates tension between academic success and time for rehearsals*), but not a more general dampening, non-supportive attitude to extra-curricular activities that was reported. Especially disappointing were comments revealing a lack of understanding of the issues raised by educational drama. A minority see it as a waste of time, just playing around, to some academic traditionalists it is of secondary importance, not recognised as an intrinsic element in the ' whole school philosophy '.

Much more encouraging were the numerous examples of positive influence reported, the support given to productions (30%) and general statements like enormous, considerable, positive (25%). Individual influence was often stressed, notably by Headteachers, other members of Senior Management Teams (*offers significant protection within non National Curriculum discretionary time*) and Heads of Faculty/Department, whose personal expertise, experience, credibility and enthusiasm could be singled out as the most important factor - *he has persuaded the staff to treat the subject with respect.* Drama is often perceived to stand, or fall, on the quality of the whole department:

- *Specialist staff pester and convince you to get what they want.*

- *Good practice has brought the staff to acknowledge drama's importance.*

Such influence should be expected, as indeed the strong support reported from many English departments, less so the frequency where consultative procedures involving a wide range of staff (Curriculum Committees, Academic Boards) had clearly decided that drama should have a high priority as an essential part of the curriculum :

- *The value of drama is recognised because Heads of Department are prepared to give up curriculum time to allow discrete delivery.*

- *Initially threatened, now supported because benefits seen.*

- *An incredibly important subject - "makes more difference than any other".*

- *Drama is considered as a key subject that is essential to all girls in this school.*

- *Members of staff in subjects other than drama are vocal in their recognition that drama and writing skills (evaluations) learned through drama have a positive effect in their subjects.*

- *All staff recognise its value for enhancing development of personal and inter-personal skills/qualities.*

- *The curriculum forum for all teaching staff created the structure, with drama well recognised as a valuable distinct area of the curriculum for all.*

- *Collectively the whole staff have developed an entitlement philosophy that includes the Creative Arts as one of its central planks.*

● IS DRAMA SEEN TO BE A VOCATIONAL SUBJECT?

Almost exactly half the 688 answers to this question said no, though some drew distinctions between the attitudes of parents, pupils and teachers, and others emphasised its intrinsic value.

- *In areas of very high unemployment it is difficult for pupils to recognise the vocational potential of any subject.*

- *Parents see drama as developing confidence, some undervalue it.*

- *Some take drama as a break from real lessons, others as a serious artistic pursuit.*

- *Seen as an Arts subject and as a personal development subject more than vocational.*

Only 12% were as unequivocal in saying yes, particularly for post-16 A Level and GNVQ courses:

- *Certainly by the less academic.*

- *Yes, but discouraged.*

- *Increasingly yes.*

- *Yes, by parents and ill-informed staff!*

The remainder were more cautious in their approach, considering the most valuable vocational element to be the spin-off as shown by personal development, confidence, team-building, taking responsibility, self esteem, all important for any career. *Drama is a life-skill for any vocation*.

A number of schools commented diversely on the extent to which drama, if not vocational, could be termed an academic subject, and its value within the curriculum.

- *Rather does it offer something of intrinsic value.*

- *Teachers see it as a major vehicle of education,* as opposed to a frivolous distraction.

- *An academic subject to support and enhance the study of English at A Level or improving skills at GCSE.*

- *The profile has been raised but still not regarded by some academic staff.*

- *Not viewed as a core subject in the curriculum.*

- *Always a tendency for more academic not to opt for drama.*

- *Academic value as well.*

- *A powerful teaching method, an authentic discipline.*

- *The subject struggles for parity with National Curriculum and more traditional subjects.*

THE HEALTH OF SCHOOL THEATRE PRODUCTIONS (See Appendix 17 and Part Four)

Productions are healthy, even excellent, in 75% of schools, unhealthy in 15% and just about keeping their head above water in the remaining 10%. More specifically :

- Productions are most at risk in single sex comprehensive and secondary modern schools.

- They are significantly healthier in independent schools, especially mixed and boys.

- The situation in grammar schools closely mirrors that in other mixed state schools, with boys' grammar schools apparently facing least problems.

- There is least ambiguity in girls' schools - they are either healthy or not.

Schools were also asked to identify the main costs and benefits of productions, and the extent of encouragement given to staff to involve themselves.

Costs

These are listed in numerical order as specifically mentioned, though some headings may refer to the same factor.

- **Staff overload.** Productions are clearly a significant pressure on all staff principally involved, a great strain on their energy, often leaving them exhausted and stressed. Comments reveal the conflict often created with other responsibilities and other colleagues.

  — *If drama staff are to be excused school-wide duties during production it equals conflict.*

  — *Increased formal responsibilities have cut staff involvement.*

  — *Staff too committed to paperwork, marking, administration, to find time and energy.*

  — *Pressure of work due to National Curriculum requirements and strong emphasis on examination outcomes are partly responsible for no school production.*

  — *Under pressure from targets, monitoring, evaluation, literacy, numeracy etc.*

  — *There are other needs to be addressed with greater priority than drama – nice to have but not essential.*

  — *There is aggravation from other colleagues over rehearsals.*

  — *Not viewed as important by drama staff (not the view of SMT) but the quality of educational drama is good.*

  — *Have to protect enthusiasts from overload.*

- **Finance.** Numerous costs were mentioned – royalties and copyright, hire of equipment, costumes, set, even accommodation, transport, caretaking, wear and tear, ensuring

Health and Safety requirements are met. Many schools feel that realistic prices cannot be charged for parents, hence a subsidy is essential, and this is a disincentive to large scale productions. Some schools paid for a significant amount of cover.

- **Time.** For both staff and students this is seen as an expensive cost, feelings best expressed by a single quotation - *the production is "ruling" the second half of the summer term.* Some schools feel productions adversely affect time for other school commitments.

- **Impact on** the curriculum and disruption to learning. Time needed for the KS3 National Curriculum, KS4 course work and other examination commitments, particularly in Year 11, is often at risk from rehearsals, most strongly put as *the whole school is turned upside down for the duration of the production.*

Difficulties

A number of schools also identified additional problems, if not precisely costs, they faced in mounting productions. Such included :

— Lack of specialist equipment, lighting etc and/or expertise to operate it,

— Competition from an increase in local youth theatre groups (sometimes seen as a strength!)

— Pressure on accommodation and facilities – loss of the school hall for a period.

— In some cases a struggle for parental support with disappointing attendance.

— *A problem to educate pupils to become good audiences.*

— Choice of productions provides interesting contrasts. By some the preference for musicals is regretted, elsewhere a more academic focus on examination texts than on pupil celebration puts other staff off. But also – *parental support weak for academic productions, strong for popular.*

— Rural transport.

After such a litany of costs and difficulties it is worth recording one school's comment under this heading – *far outweighed by the benefits!,* which are now identified below.

Benefits

As with costs it is difficult accurately to compartmentalise all the benefits - many overlap. Many were general statements like *huge, immense, priceless, unique, endless, a forever experience.* From others one could detect five broad groups, listed in order as above:

- **Publicity, prestige and public relations.** Unsurprisingly the principal example given was liaison with feeder schools and parents, a strong vehicle for recruitment. Productions are seen as – *a good shop window,* as ensuring – *good word of mouth recommendations on the grapevine.*

- **Pupil involvement.** The range of benefits identified for individual pupils included confidence, self-esteem, a sense of belonging and identity, and sheer enjoyment.

  Means of personal, social and educational growth.

  Great value for disaffected, low achieving pupils.

  Gives status to some boys in a strong sports school.

  Often the most positive experience in the school career of some children.

  Arguably one of the most memorable and potentially transforming experience of their school life.

  Highlight of the drama year and a memory of the school that stays with students long after thay have left - of inestimable educational worth.

- **Staff/pupil co-operation.** Typical phrases that occurred frequently were *esprit de corps, a focus for collegiality and togetherness,* and the *feel good factor.* Productions give a school '*buzz'.*

  Staff want to be involved with pupils, though difficult to convince all staff of how pupils benefit.

  New staff see productions as a means of getting to know students on a different level.

  Staff see them as the best way of becoming friends and advocates of pupils.

- **Relationships with parents and the wider community.** As for prospective, so for current parents and the community at large, productions are seen as an important encouragement to support and take pride in the school.

A visible showcase for the excellence of mainstream drama work.

- **School ethos.** summing up all the views above, productions are seen as an essential part of a rich school life.

Staff support

Be it costs and difficulties or benefits, staff are a key ingredient, hence this final issue. A previous section reported staff influence on drama including the level of support given to productions. Under this heading more details are given, the only common factor being how variable the situation is, even within the same school.

Encouragement is certainly needed. Problems identified where voluntary assistance has declined included:

- Age – *limited sign of young staff coming through to take the place of dynamos running down.*

- Other staff being too busy with administration, their own subjects or commitment to other responsibilities.

- Even specialists not believing it to be their role to deliver productions – *the curriculum most important – the production is a totally separate discrete event.* But the importance of the enthusiasm and motivating power of the drama specialist is constantly stressed.

Particular stress was laid on possible inducements, with conflicting views:

- *No pay, no help.*

- *No time and money, but the issue has been debated.*

- *Play rehearsals out of school but no recognition in time in other respects.*

- *No inducements or incentives deemed necessary.*

Clearly vital is the role of Head, Senior Management Team and Governors in giving encouragement. By the ethos of some schools *staff are expected to be involved in some sort of extra-curricular activity.* Heads encouraged others by giving time for rehearsals – an extreme example being *pupils and staff off timetable for one week – £1000 support.* Crucially all staff participation, as in any other aspect of school life, must be positively recognised. It is the Heads' principal task to ensure their own enthusiasm permeates the staff.

It was pleasing to read that personal interest and self-satisfaction were often the only motivation needed for staff - *the high level of staff commitment an inspiration to students.* Young staff felt it was good for their c.v. But finally it was most encouraging where the greatest satisfaction for staff lay in the success and enthusiasm of students:

- *the only encouragement is the enthusiasm of students.*

- *the only motivation for staff is the pleasure derived from a communal artistic endeavour and watching children succeed.*

With such attitudes the future health of the majority of school productions is surely in good hands.

Peter Miller, in his foreword, identified a number of important issues regarding the current state of drama in secondary schools and colleges, both within and beyond the timetabled curriculum. Should it be in the National Curriculum? Is too much attention paid to productions to the detriment of educational drama? How well used is drama as a vehicle for personal development? Are teachers of drama sufficiently well qualified for the task they face? Does this survey confirm or deny such concerns? Readers will draw their own conclusions, but the following seem to be the principal conclusions that can be drawn and questions that remain:

- Despite all the difficulties drama is well established in the majority of schools and colleges.

- Though it may be sensible for drama to be set within an Arts Faculty, there should always be a specialist Head of Department.

- Drama, no less than any other subject, requires fully qualified **specialist** teachers.

- It cannot be automatically assumed that drama can be taught either within the English curriculum or by English teachers.

- The Teacher Training Agency proposals for diluting Initial Teacher Training requirements for drama should not be implemented – more specialism is needed, not less.

- Provision of well-equipped specialist accommodation should have a higher priority – far too often effective delivery is hampered by inadequate rooming/hall arrangements.

- Local Authorities should also more fully recognise the role they have, through funding and advisory services, for promoting drama in schools.

- There should be more consistency in the priority given to drama.

- In the light of drama's positive impact on literacy through oracy it would be shortsighted and counter-productive to reduce curriculum time for drama in order to make room for other literacy work.

- In curriculum planning at KS 3 & 4 drama should be recognised for having as valuable a contribution to make to academic and personal development as any other subject – indeed it is an essential element.

CONCLUSIONS

- GCSE syllabuses need constant scrutiny to ensure that the assessment procedures are relevant to the subject.

- Extra-curricular drama is flourishing, with a wide range of activities, through the enthusiasm, energy and commitment of both specialist and non-specialist staff.

- The success of extra-curricular drama should not submerge the crucial contribution that educational drama makes to pupil development. Each school should seek to have an appropriate balance between them.

- When drama is used more widely by non-specialist staff, relevant in-service training should be provided.

- The all-embracing benefits that drama brings to pupils' personal and social development include important vocational elements, encouraging qualities valuable in any pupil's future.

- When difficult staffing/accommodation decisions have to be taken the support of well-briefed governors is vital.

- Schools should encourage all staff to recognise the value that both educational drama and theatre productions bring to individual pupils and the full life of the community.

- Though whole staff support is important, even more critical is individual expertise, enthusiasm and commitment, coupled with vision from the Headteacher.

- The valuable contribution that school productions make to the ethos of the school and the pupils involved is obvious – thus it is important that the whole process is **well-managed** in terms of time and the strain and stress on staff minimised.

- **The final conclusion must be that drama's omission from the National Curriculum is universally held responsible for any decrease, failure to increase, lack of priority and most of the difficulties outlined in the survey. Many of the issues above would be resolved if *Drama was a National Curriculum subject in its own right.* But even here a word of caution is appropriate — might creativity then be stifled by over-prescription?**

    A school without drama is a school without a soul!

PART
2

DRAMA IN
SCHOOLS TODAY —
THE CASE STUDIES

● INTRODUCTION

The Case Studies which follow are all written by Heads, Deputy Heads and teachers who kindly volunteered to share the experiences of their schools and colleges. They stand 'in their own right' with minimal editing.

It became clear as we read the questionnaire responses that there was a considerable richness of good and interesting practice. Our problem was to select from these riches. We have tried to present examples from around the UK and from all types of secondary school: state and independent, selective and comprehensive, mixed and single-sex, from affluent and deprived areas.

We hope that all readers will find examples from which they will gain ideas, food for thought, reassurance and perhaps some fun. Some concentrate on drama within the curriculum, some more on extra curricular drama - some of it quite spectacular. They include travel with the writers into Europe, to the Edinburgh festival and to a joint drama club with the nearby blind school! And how about a production involving children from 23 different schools?

In several cases the writers emphasise the potential effect of good drama on the whole school - it can even be dramatic (!) as in the case of Glan Ely School, where the Head partially ascribes the school's escape from 'special measures' to the new drama provision. The influence can go even wider, of course, as in the Bexleyheath Arts Festival. Other writers, as the author of the Sir Graham Balfour School entry, argue fiercely that drama should be maintained as a separate organisational entity, and not be lost within a larger faculty such as English. Others again pursue the importance of links with PSE and the development of pupils' emotional literacy through drama. The theme which probably recurs most often, however, is the importance of the *people* concerned - the active support of senior staff and governors, added to the impact of enthusiastic staff supported by willing parents - real partnerships in action for the benefit of the young people in their schools.

● ARTS FESTIVAL
Bexleyheath School, London Borough of Bexley

CELEBRATING EUROPE WITH SOCRATES:
THE COLNE IN EUROPE
Colne Community School, Colchester

ROLE OF DRAMA IN A 'FAILING' SCHOOL
Glan Ely High School, Cardiff

USE OF NEW WRITING
Hasland Hall Community School, Chesterfield

A DRAMA DEPARTMENT COMPLIMENTED BY OFSTED
Mortimer Comprehensive School, South Shields

TREADING THE BOARDS WITHOUT TREADING ON TOES —
THE SCHOOL PLAY
Omagh Academy, Northern Ireland

GCSE AND PERFORMANCE DRAMA IN AN INDEPENDENT
BOYS' COMPREHENSIVE
Sandbach School, Cheshire

JOINT DRAMA CLUB, SIGHTED AND BLIND
St Margaret's School and The Royal Blind School, Edinburgh

A MONSTER PRODUCTION
Sir Frank Markham Community School, Milton Keynes

RE-LAUNCHING DRAMA IN A COMPREHENSIVE
Sir Graham Balfour School, Stafford

THE AESTHETICS FEDERATION
Waddesdon C. of E. School, Nr Aylesbury, Bucks

EDINBURGH EXPERIENCES
Wey Valley School, Weymouth

THE YEAR 9 PRODUCTION
The Grammar School for Girls, Wilmington, Kent

DRAMA IN A RURAL BOARDING GM SCHOOL
Wymondham College, Norfolk

ARTS FESTIVAL

BEXLEYHEATH SCHOOL,
LONDON BOROUGH OF BEXLEY

BEXLEYHEATH SCHOOL

We are a mixed school serving all abilities in Bexley, on the edge of London, quite close to the Dartford River Crossing and the county of Kent. We have around 1800 pupils aged 11 to 19, taught in our lower, upper and sixth form campuses. We are committed to the arts as important for all young people. The Arts Festival allows all subject disciplines to make a contribution to learning in the arts. It also promotes learning in the arts as extending beyond the boundaries of the school, taking advantage of opportunities provided by, for example, the South Bank Centre and the Globe in London.

Where we started

Lucy James, an English teacher, was appointed Festival Co-ordinator in the autumn of 1995. She and her Area Manager, Keith Hammond, had the task of setting up the Festival for June 1996. The aims were:-

1. to provide a range of arts experiences for all children in and out of school;

2. to provide children with access to writers, performers, artists and others working in the arts;

3. to connect with Bexleyheath Town Centre Partnership;

4. to link the arts with European awareness;

5. to include our Year 7 Environment Day;

6. to involve at least 1000 primary children.

What we did

The Festival was scheduled for two weeks in June. The work developed on a slow burning fuse. It was always behind time and above budget. The governors' marketing committee agreed to meet administrative costs. We are a British Telecom-sponsored school and they agreed to be our main Festival sponsor. The other was our own Parents Association. Businesses from the Town

Partnership sponsored individual events. The Partnership handled the arrangements for performances in the shopping centre. The Festival team involved representatives from every department in the school. They would all run events linked to their own subjects during the Festival. The Festival brochure was funded by Bexley Council.

Festival 1996 and 1997

Roger McGough OBE launched the 1996 Festival and 500 balloons in front of the Mayor and the whole school. There were over three hundred events. Visitors included the Globe players, Roy Apps, (writer of 'Byker Grove'), and the Japanese Festival Trust, The Goethe Institute, a visit by students from our German partner school and a French café run by staff and pupils provided a strong European dimension. We held a music recital at our local church and parents attended our drama production and other events. The 1997 Festival was run on similar lines but on a larger scale. It involved many visits to Europe including a cross - curricular Fine Art and Languages week in Provence.

Festival 1998

Following a rigorous evaluation we plan a series of improvements designed to upgrade the quality of the Festival. Details are still under wraps. Only the main school production, 'The Lion, The Witch and The Wardrobe' run by our sixth form Performing Arts group has been advertised so far. As to the future, we are working with the Council and the Town Centre Partnership to promote the Festival as a community event. A recent report on the future of the Bexleyheath town centre envisages a big rôle for our Festival in building on the success of the area as one of London's most successful centres.

Malcolm Noble

Head Teacher

CELEBRATING EUROPE WITH SOCRATES: THE COLNE IN EUROPE

COLNE COMMUNITY SCHOOL, COLCHESTER

A four-way Expressive Arts and language development initiative

SOCRATES: **1996: EUROPEAN REVOLUTION**

                               1997: FUTURE VISIONS

                               1998: DESTINATION ITALY

European Work/Background to the Socrates Project

Over the past eight years the Colne Community School has been transformed from a good secondary school to a good European Secondary School. The school has always had visits abroad, the first Exchange of students taking place between the Colne and a Gymnasium in Marne, Schleswig-Holstein in 1990. From this point in time, the school has never looked back. We have highly successful German and French Exchanges, Sixth Form Work Experience in France and Germany and Year 8 Study visits to France and Germany. The school started to take in European Sixth Formers in 1994 and they have played a large rôle in breaking down barriers between the countries and allowing students throughout the school to see for themselves that we are one Europe.

The year 1994 was a watershed for us. In that year we linked up with the Lycée Européen in Villers-Cotterêts with the aim of providing "cultural exchanges". The aim was to involve one department per year and as many students as possible in a faculty-based project on a chosen theme. The project in 1994 was co-ordinated by the Head of French in conjunction with the Humanities Faculty. Students have visited Brightlingsea for a short period each year from 1994 to work with English students on a research project followed by a final presentation of their work.

The Lycée has also been twinned with a Gymnasium in Essen, Germany, for some time and in September 1995 we were asked to become involved with both schools in a project part-funded via the Socrates Programme. We jumped at the chance, as did two Italian schools contacted by the Gymnasium. The five of us set ourselves targets and these were surpassed in October 1996 with our first Expressive Arts Extravaganza. In 1997 we built on our successes through even closer collaboration.

Socrates: Initial Work: Planning and getting started

Preparatory work for the October 1996 project began in Villers-Cotterêts, France, in November 1995, when staff involved decided on the angle the project would take. It was decided that the best way to demonstrate collaboration and unity was to put on a revue so that everyone could see the message we were trying to spread. Hence the Expressive Arts would be the vehicle for our European interaction. The title in 1996 was "European Revolution".

In March 1996 representatives from each country (and the Headteachers of all but one school) met in Essen Germany to feed back ideas and decide on the plan of action. The UK school had the dramatic expertise, so advice would come from here. The job of linking the plays together in a satisfactory manner would also fall to the UK with support from the other countries of course (clearly, this was the only way we could work given the absence of Drama as a curriculum subject on the continent).

There are/were many aims and objectives ; three important ones for our school are:

1. To give students in the Performing Arts area of the curriculum the opportunity to fulfil the criteria for their "A" level course.

2. To produce a Performing Arts Module with a European flavour which can be incorporated into the Schemes of Work of Years 11 & 12, thus enriching the existing curriculum for many students.

3. To allow students (all of whom have studied languages) the opportunity to be immersed in foreign languages for one week.

Sign language and song are wonderful ways of communicating.

The activities and their impact

Throughout each project year, the partnership schools have exchanged ideas and set their students to work writing original sketches and, for 1997, original music.

The progression was from "European Revolution" to "Future Visions". (Next year will be a further progression to "Destination Italy"). The only way forward has been to rehearse as individual schools up until the final workshop and performance, when the sketches and plays have been linked together through integrated activities. We have established a tradition of students themselves taking the lead, choreographing and working out their own links in a professional and responsible manner. We see the workshop as the key to the whole project; here we are as one nation - yet at the same time speaking different languages, adapting and changing plays, learning to compromise and generally interacting with each other. Sign language and song are wonderful ways of communicating. The language development is inherent in the workshop/rehearsal programme. The links between the plays/ sketches have been particularly rewarding and a major challenge, partially due to the numbers: 55 students were involved in 1996 and, including technical staff, 100 in 1997. These links have been produced through improvisation; there is no script, but simply a structure for the performance evening.

At present, students are preparing for the final Socrates year when we hope to go to Italy. "Destination Italy " will consist of a broad selection of music, drama, dance and literature. This will use improvisation, rehearsal and performance. We hope to continue our joint project work beyond the 3-year duration of Socrates.

"The quality of the performance is important: however, it is the cumulative process of workshop and rehearsal which brings into play the necessary communication skills of our language development project SOCRATES."(John Collins, Head of Drama, Colne Community School).

J.P. Else, European Co-ordinator

[Editor's note:

There are videos of 'Essen 1996' and 'Future Visions'. Contact the school for further details.]

ROLE OF DRAMA IN A 'FAILING' SCHOOL

GLAN ELY HIGH SCHOOL, CARDIFF

The Context

Glan Ely High School is an 11-18 comprehensive school in Cardiff serving an area of real deprivation, more famous for its riots than its academic prowess. In 1995 it was inspected and found to be failing to provide a proper standard of education for its pupils. A follow up inspection by H.M.I. confirmed the initial findings.

All the classic symptoms of failing schools were present, ranging from financial management and planning to poor standards in the classroom. Exclusions were very high (over 150) and exam results low (5 A* to C pass rate of 4%). The school had been the subject of a considerable amount of speculation in the years building up to the inspection and a plan for reorganisation has very recently been turned down. A Deputy had been acting Head for almost two years.

Staff at the school faced many difficulties – low levels of parental support (the meeting to consider the Action Plan attracted only 6 parents) ; long standing patterns of poor attendance (Year 10 had recently been at 54%); lack of resources (the only network of computers in the school was one of 10 year old 186 machines). Among the greatest problems facing staff, however, was the very low levels of literacy skills. (In last year's Year 7 only 5 out of 134 pupils had reading ages at or above their chronological age.)

The Action Plan

It was decided right away that the LEA would do whatever was necessary to turn this situation around. A very detailed action plan was devised. The Governing Body was increased by the addition of several people with a range of specialist expertise. An experienced Headteacher was appointed. A totally new management structure was put into place. A significant sum of money was made available to establish the school as a Centre of Excellence in engineering.

The Role of Drama

In a situation such as this there are a number of steps that can be taken. Underpinning all actions was a theme of raising self belief – for staff and parents as well as for pupils. The plan for the Centre of Excellence was modified to become a Centre of Excellence in the Media. This was developed because it would provide a vehicle for setting up situations in which the role of Drama could come more to the fore. Moreover, a Senior Manager, who had recently been Head of English and Drama was appointed with the title Literacy Co-ordinator.

Drama was seen as a strong subject at the school. Value added analyses of GCSE results showed that it was an area where pupils at the school did comparatively well. It was also one that was viewed positively by pupils. The annual Showtime event was one of the few occasions that filled the Hall with parents. The Media centre was seen as a vehicle to pull Drama from its ghetto position and put it right into the middle of the turn around in the school's fortunes.

The reason for this choice was the belief that Drama had a unique role to play in developing not only the pupils' literacy skills, but also their confidence and self belief. For generations the school's catchment had been associated with failure. As part of a wider package of measures to work on this issue Drama was seen as a potent force in allowing the pupils to develop their communication skills one step removed from their own situation. This took away the sense of threat and the negative relationships that pertained.

For pupils who are able to move from one speech code to another without giving a second thought, there might be no need to set up false situations to encourage it. In this part of Cardiff, however, you need to 'pretend'. Newscasts had to be set up to develop formal language, without threatening their local dialect.

The Tactics

Drama as a subject is compulsory for all pupils in Key Stage 3. It is an option in Key Stage 4 and a Theatre Studies A level is about to be introduced. This was not, however, the key thrust. Instead the tactic of using Drama as a teaching strategy in other areas of the curriculum is being developed. The Head of Drama provided INSET for staff as a whole. The curriculum was modified such that the first month of Year 7 was set aside for Literacy Development. A key element of this was the use of Drama techniques to develop oracy.

In History, the reporting back of understanding took the form of producing a radio and TV broadcast from the 'Battle of Hastings'. In French, the development of language was reinforced by the production of a play with pupils taking on various classroom roles (including teacher) and then studying the video made in order to evaluate their performance.

This approach was developed in other contexts. In Geography, Year 9 pupils worked on putting together their own video programme for the topic on Brazil. In PSE there have been several instances of the use of drama to develop the ability to accept (and the skills to give) peer criticism in non threatening situations. In Music, the performance skills have been enhanced to support the musical skills. Pupils were recently featured on National TV and Radio as they 'performed' the latest recording on their own Record Label. The school has termly award ceremonies and a former pupil and well known TV actress were invited to attend and to then give a workshop on dramatic techniques.

Developments

There are plans in hand for much greater structured use of Drama. The Head of Drama has been allocated time each week specifically for 'Curriculum Enhancement'. As well as the GCSE Drama course in Key Stage 4 the timetable for next year will have a 'Communications Technology' course as part of the compulsory core for all pupils, leading towards the award of a Youth Awards Scheme accreditation. A radio recording studio is now available to students as part of the new Media Centre and digital editing of both video and sound is about to be installed.

The Results

It is always difficult to isolate any single component in anything as complex as a school. Certainly there have been many other changes at the school during the last couple of years. Drama was seen however, as a way to bring about certain key changes. These included:

- Improvements in motivation.

- Increases in literacy levels.

- Greater confidence and self belief.

- More involvement from parents.

- Changes in teaching strategies across the curriculum.

- Examples of excellence to act as 'targets'.

All of this, it was hoped, would lead to improved examination results

It is now just over two years from the initial Inspection report. The GCSE pass rate last summer was 15% 5 A* to C. The attendance is up by 5% compared to last year. The last parents evening was standing room only. The pupils requested and designed their own new uniform with the logo of a 'Big G' representing the turnaround. In a national survey of pupil attitudes those at Glan Ely showed consistently improving attitudes towards school.

In January 1998 the school was taken off the Special Measures list.

Peter Leech

Headteacher

USE OF
NEW WRITING

HASLAND HALL COMMUNITY SCHOOL, CHESTERFIELD

New Writing in Curriculum Drama

Original performance work within the Drama curriculum has evolved partly as a response to the increased difficulty of funding TIE from external companies, and partly as a logical development of the work already undertaken in school.

'Charlotte Corday'. We are in the process of developing a performance piece for a Year 8 audience that will help to deliver the French Revolution module within Humanities. Year 9 students are helping to devise and will perform the 'play'.

'Anti-Bullying'. GCSE Drama students are involved in devising and delivering a performance / workshop TIE package for primary schools (Years 5 & 6). This is funded by the Derbyshire LEA Reducing Truancy Project. We also hope to perform to Year 7 students at Hasland Hall, and there will be a public 'showcase' giving an opportunity for parents and other members of staff to view the work.

New Writing in Extra-Curricular / Performance Work

1. 'The Land Where No-One Ever Dies' : storytelling theatre. Devised with, and by, Year 8 students. Based on a traditional story. Performed with 'Lost Cause?'

   'Lost Cause?' : a devised piece based on a newspaper story. It involved Year 10 students and was performed as part of an Expressive Arts 'evening'.

2. 'Partners in Time' : a full scale production. Students came up with initial ideas (an adventure / romance that was "happy", "funny" and "exciting", set in the past, present and future – no problem!). I went away and devised a plot outline with an episodic structure. This meant we could assign responsibility for writing separate sections of the play to different teams of students. Each section was more or less self-contained. I wrote the links, and the beginning and ending. Nearly a dozen students were involved as writers, and well over 50 in performance, design and technical roles.

3. 'Cuba', by Liz Lochhead (the only piece written by 'an outsider'). Part of the BT/National Theatre 'National Connections' Project. 12 brand new plays for young people were commissioned by the National. Each of the schools and youth theatres selected chose one to produce. Weekend workshops were held for the directors (with writers and regional theatres), funded by the project. We performed 'Cuba', very successfully, at Hasland Hall. Assessors from the National and Sheffield Crucible Theatre came to see the production and we were lucky enough to be invited to perform at the Crucible. This was an exciting experience. One of the students described it as "the best day of her life". We performed to an audience of 450.

4. 'About Face' – new play written by me. In this we are exploring issues of identity, mental health, families and friendship. I am trying to build on some of the experiences / techniques we developed when working on 'Cuba', and to explore themes of relevance to our students and school.

Planned Future Projects

1. We will apply to be involved in the next round of 'National Connections'.

2. Performance project with Science, possibly for presentation to primary schools, exploring Cosmology.

3. Extra-curricular : next year is the 350th anniversary of the Diggers 'social experiment' at the end of the English Civil War. We explore this in Y8 Drama, so I'm thinking of preparing a piece that links the historical narrative with contemporary 'protest' movements.

The 'policy' of performing only new work has evolved; it wasn't something I dogmatically set out to do. There are clear advantages, however. No copyright; you are always breaking new ground (which is appreciated by staff, parents and, particularly, students); you can ensure the work is exciting, challenging and appropriate for the particular students involved; it releases the creativity of staff and students. I think it's good for students to see that their Drama teacher is not just expecting creativity and imagination from them, but can produce it himself – whilst at the same time not imposing on them but offering a structured framework for their own creative and inventive energy.

The original work we have undertaken has had a positive effect on curricular Drama (including exam results). Students involved as performers have become increasingly willing to take imaginative 'risks' and have developed innovative, exciting work of their own. Student audiences have been given a 'model' of what it is possible to achieve through Drama and this has inspired and motivated their own work within lessons.

I am hoping that benefits will become increasingly tangible throughout the school and across the curriculum as we develop further cross-curricular projects.

Paul Whitfield

Asst. Head of Expressive Arts

(Teacher of Drama)

A DRAMA DEPARTMENT COMPLIMENTED BY OFSTED

MORTIMER COMPREHENSIVE SCHOOL, SOUTH SHIELDS

Drama at Mortimer is delivered as an integrated part of the Performing Arts - incorporating dance, drama and music. Although these are taught as discrete subjects they are grouped together for the purposes of administration, planning, organisation, assessment and reporting. In addition a common methodology has been developed and common themes are explored in all areas.

Planning is multi-layered whereby themes of work are displayed on half-termly planning sheets but also broken down into lesson by lesson sections with specific learning outcomes clearly identified. This enables continuity within the work whilst also giving teachers freedom to vary approaches according to teaching styles and individual classes.

Units of work are reviewed annually and positive development of content and approaches is enabled through a process of evaluation. Carefully planned progression is an important aspect of drama work across the lower school years. This includes progression in both course content and what is expected of pupils in the level and quality of their response - a response measured against clearly defined assessment criteria.

The work in Year Seven concentrates on enabling pupils to acquire the basic skills needed to invent and extend ideas. They are introduced to the arts process of making, presenting, responding and evaluating. Activities introducing pupils to simple listening and speaking situations, adopting a role, creating and structuring improvisation, responding to others and to the teacher in role are a central part of the course. These are then structured to develop confidence, communication skills and social skills.

Pupils in Year 10 and 11 must study at least one arts subject, including visual arts, at G.C.S.E. level.

Departmental planning consciously recognises the need to give Year Eight pupils the opportunity to respond to a wide range of stimuli and to develop their own ideas in increasing depth. This allows firm consolidation of the skills developed in year seven. Structure, as a means of clearly communicating ideas, becomes a focus of the class work and pupils are encouraged to perform to others with confidence.

In Year Nine the work acknowledges the increasing maturity of the pupils and this is reflected in the themes chosen – such as the pressures of adolescence. Conveyance of feeling and emotions, using an increasing range of drama structures and techniques, is the focus of the work during this year. Further study of the work of Shakespeare is built into the Year Nine course and this supports the work of the English Department in preparing for Key Stage 3 S.A.T.S. Pupils are given the opportunity to develop both competence and confidence in their use of the drama skills and are encouraged to produce work of an accomplished standard as preparation for the forthcoming G.C.S.E. courses.

Pupils in Year 10 and 11 must study at least one arts subject, including visual arts, at G.C.S.E. level. Pupils opting for Drama follow the N.E.A.B. syllabus concentrating on improvisation and scripted performance.

To complement and support work within the department theatre visits are organised and pupils are given as many opportunities as possible to work with visiting artists.

Bernie Boyle

Head of Performing Arts

[Editor's note:

The work of this drama department was complimented by Ofsted for the quality of its work and its rigorous organisation and teaching methods.]

TREADING THE BOARDS WITHOUT TREADING ON TOES — THE SCHOOL PLAY

OMAGH ACADEMY, NORTHERN IRELAND

Over the years, Omagh Academy has built up a fine reputation in staging good school plays. However, there is no rigid formula for producing and staging a successful school play, especially since success tends to emanate from steady evolution and a fresh approach each year. Nevertheless, the conventions which have been established underpin continued excellence in this field.

The choice of play is made early in the first term by the Head of English and Drama and this is followed by careful auditions beginning in the second week of term and lasting up to two weeks. The success of a school production is largely dependent upon suitable casting, and rigorous auditions are a feature of the process. Without delay the new cast is thrust into an intensive rehearsal schedule, including daily rehearsals in the lunch hour, with practices after school and on Saturdays as necessary. In addition, a precondition to joining the cast is a willingness to attend rehearsals during mid-term break at Halloween. Such is the rehearsal programme that the cast is quickly familiarised with the play, the characters and setting, and each actor is encouraged to explore all aspects of the role he or she is playing.

The Academy play may begin in the English Department but the cast soon enlist the support of many other pupils, teachers and departments. The Art and Technology departments take charge of directing students in set-design and construction (which may be undertaken as subject coursework). The Home Economics department lends support in costume design and speciality music requirements are researched by the Music department. The sound and lighting crew is managed by a number of staff from the Science Department and the Parents' Association helps with stage furniture and other props. Programmes are designed under the supervision of the school's I.T. specialists. In this way the Academy play develops into a real "school" production as pupils with their varying talents and skills make an active contribution to the production alongside members of staff and parents.

Even the direction of the production is shouldered in large measure by students who certainly benefit from their experiences in terms of both drama and general team work. Intensive rehearsals take place in the final, stressful week before the opening performances. During "Playweek" the school accepts a degree of disruption to normal timetable activities as pupils are excused from class for final rehearsals, and putting the finishing touches to the set. Evening performances draw the support of many members of staff who come in to assist with make-up and help with front of house operations such as welcoming visitors. Sherry is served in the staff room before curtain-up by the community on two nights with the rest of the week given over to performances for local schools. Academy pupils themselves, in conjunction with the English department, review the play as class projects. Publicity in the local press along with effective poster advertising ensures good public audiences for the evening performances. Reviews in the local papers have been consistently complimentary about the high standards achieved by the actors and production teams.

Success has encouraged the choice of challenging plays by the Academy's producer-director, which have included the compelling Arthur Miller play "The Crucible", Sean O'Casey's "Juno and The Paycock", and most recently, the Tennessee Williams classic, "A Streetcar Named Desire".

However, no play is without its critics and this year the Headmaster received a comment from a member of the Board of Governors that "A Streetcar Named Desire" was too strong a play for Sixth Formers and wholly inappropriate viewing for First Formers. The first step in producing a school play is clearly choosing a title!

Michael Murphy

Head of English / Drama

GCSE AND PERFORMANCE DRAMA IN AN INDEPENDENT BOYS' COMPREHENSIVE

SANDBACH SCHOOL, CHESHIRE

At Sandbach School, drama is represented at KS3 in a Performing Arts Carousel, at KS4 by the NEAB GCSE syllabus, and at 16+ by Performing Arts A-level; production drama lies within the remit of the Drama department as "Sandbach School Theatre".

Drama at KS4 – N.E.A.B. Syllabus

Drama appears in one option column for GCSE and numbers have varied from 15 to 35 (involving team teaching) in recent years; the average intake would be 20-25. Year 10 is viewed as an opportunity to develop an in-depth skills base across the areas of scripted performance; improvisation and set design/lighting. The areas of properties and costume/make-up on the NEAB syllabus are not attempted. Consequently, by the end of year 10 pupils have experienced a wide range of scripts and are familiar with the structural demands of polished improvisation. Whilst all pupils are given a grounding in technical skills, a significant few develop these to a high level of expertise - drawing on IT skills for lighting and sound control for in-class and public performances. A philosophy of 'empowerment' exists to allow those with technical expertise to develop it to the full.

In performance areas at GCSE, a critical evaluation of performance is instilled from the start of year 10 in both self and in others; initial performances may be confined to the group and later are extended to lunchtime performances open to the school. By year 11 all performance practicals are before an open audience of parents, staff and peers. The **performance process** is seen to be at the heart of success at GCSE. After Whit in year 10 pupils opt for two of the three skill areas and choose one for their coursework (until December of Year 11) and the other for their controlled test (Feb/March Year 11); hence a critical awareness and skills base derived from Year 10 work is vital to ensure success in a controlled test situation.

Sandbach School Theatre

This has become well-established over the past decade and has received national acclaim for work with new writing. Through the BT National Connections scheme for new writing, SST has been showcased at the Royal National Theatre twice in the last three years, first with a school-commissioned play "Roaring Boys" in 1994, and last summer with an all-male 'Peking Opera' version of a radical feminist new play 'More Light'. 'More Light' is currently being re-rehearsed to tour to Germany in May 1998 at the invitation of the Junges Staats Theater Wiesbaden via the RNT. Touring has been a recent development for Sandbach School Theatre - Roaring Boys toured in 1994 to Portsmouth, Manchester City of Drama Festival and the Edinburgh Festival Fringe. A large scale tour of "The Royal Hunt of the Sun" is currently being planned for October 1999 to Hong Kong, having recently received an invitation to perform at the Hong Kong Youth Arts Festival. Touring inevitably involves much fund-raising - organised through parental support groups. Since 1994 over £20,000 has been raised by local fund-raising and business sponsorship to allow SST to take productions of the highest quality on tour. SST has featured regularly and positively in the national press for its initiatives.

Over the years, no set pattern for production drama has evolved. Usually there are two productions per year, and numerous single evenings of performance drama; on average a large-scale musical is produced once every three years. The unifying features of all SST work is a commitment to high standards of performance and technical back-up and a continuum of challenging texts: recent examples include "Equus" "Amadeus" "Rosencrantz and Guildenstern are Dead" and "Lord of the Flies". Since 1994 the trend of production drama has been towards physical theatre and stylised performance, with dance having been successfully introduced at this all-boys school. Whilst the drama department is not part of a faculty structure, it links in readily with Dance, Music and Art departmental contributions to produce theatre of the highest order yet retaining accessibility within the context of a comprehensive school.

W.J. Lonsdale
Head of Drama
C.R. Brown
Head Teacher

...with dance having been success-fully introduced at this all-boys school.

63

JOINT DRAMA CLUB, SIGHTED AND BLIND

ST MARGARET'S SCHOOL AND THE ROYAL BLIND SCHOOL, EDINBURGH

Teaching at The Royal Blind School, Edinburgh, I am acutely aware of the importance of Drama. The pupils of the school, primary and secondary, have various visual impairments and learning support needs, but are extremely enthusiastic in drama class. Class sizes are small and are carefully planned around the specific requirements of the children who are given appropriate classroom support. Drama is a way of extending their experience which is much narrower than that of a mainstream pupil. It offers children another way of making sense of their world by building on their creativity and imagination. It enables them to experience new things in a fun way and to practise real life situations and scenarios that the rest of us take for granted.

I felt that Drama was a perfect way to move forward and forge links with other schools. I was also teaching at St. Margaret's - an all girls' private school – at this time. The Drama Department was just beginning to take off with the introduction of Standard Grade exam classes. The girls are bright, energetic and enjoyed the practical aspects of drama. However ... a different world from the RBS. And so in Spring, 1996, the new joint Drama Club was set up.

I was quite nervous on that first spring afternoon when 10 pupils from St. Margaret's and 10 from the RBS met at 4 p.m. in the gym. However, simple practical solutions soon presented themselves to any problems I might have foreseen. Each group with no briefing from me accepted the other in a very natural way. Problems that I had anticipated proved unfounded. One boy has no legs and requested to be out of his wheelchair for the activities. His group took this in their stride and whoever worked or chatted with him simply sat on the floor.

When teaching Drama to blind and visually impaired children, it is necessary to rethink and adapt material to make it relevant. Mirroring exercises, for example, mean nothing to blind children but when palms are touching and the pupils move, concentrating on who is leading, changing the leadership, making controlled movements with slow music suggesting specific moods, the exercise makes sense. The joint club gave an opportunity for lots of new experimentation in movement and expression.

I had wondered about the "hands-on" approach that would be necessary in activities. Physical contact can be quite intimidating especially if you are a 13 year old girl who has just been partnered with a 16 year old blind boy. Again, through discussion and activity, the groups communicated and got to know each other. I was surprised how quickly they appeared to be comfortable with one another. Only one girl expressed reservations later and said that she sometimes felt "fussed over" and a little intimidated. This was clearly something that I had to watch for and address as it happened. Another worry was the relevance of freeze frame movement to blind pupils. Through work done at the Drama Club I learned just how exciting and relevant this kind of experience can be.

Our starting point was some storytelling. We chose to begin with the rather gruesome (true) local story of "Burke and Hare" who murdered unfortunate waifs and strays around the streets of Edinburgh and sold their bodies to the Medical School. In the context of this story we began talking about "dramatic expression" - feeling one another's faces and talking about what looks good to the audience and what feels good for the actor. So much of our facial expression and body language is learned through sight that it is sometimes difficult to explain to a blind child why they should stand or move in a certain way. Groups worked closely together explaining everything as they went along. We discussed how people moved, stood and walked. Discussion was the key at this stage. We built up a series of freeze-frames (frozen pictures) high-lighting dramatic moments within the story. It was important that each pupil knew exactly what was happening at this stage, where they were in relation to one another in terms of levels, distancing, space and what their relationship was to one another. When this was clear and the pupils could answer questions in role, we developed the freeze frames into scenes and created a play.

Having had experience of teaching both groups separately I was able to observe any differences in their performance. The RBS pupils were working with greater pace and a more creative way - obviously finding the visitors' presence challenging. The involvement of St. Margaret's meant that the blind and visually impaired pupils had guidance and support within the drama. They didn't need a teacher or classroom assistant to give any physical help. Because support came from within the drama, it wasn't intrusive. The St. Margaret's girls worked in a different way finding answers to practical problems and developing language skills. They had to use language in a more precise way. "You go there" wasn't enough.

One of the most rewarding aspects of the club was the social interaction that took place. The young people made friends and bantered about teachers, schools and the ever-present Premier League! It is pleasant to bump into a loitering St. Margaret's girl in the corridor the odd evening because she has "just come to visit".

The joint drama club was an excellent confidence building exercise and clearly boosted the self-esteem of all the young people involved. By the end of the second term they had come to trust and accept each other. In fact the acceptance was such that the St. Margaret's girls sometimes forgot and had to be reminded that some of the cast were blind. This development suggested that these young people would not grow up with the misconceptions and fears that some adults harbour about disability.

The joint group performed at a very successful entertainments evening for friends and family and continue to meet each week. Further links have been developed with other Secondary and Primary Departments and are proving to be positive, exciting, creative fun.

Aine T. Murphy

Drama Teacher, Royal Blind School.

Joy, and disaster! All the middle schools wanted to take part.

A MONSTER PRODUCTION

SIR FRANK MARKHAM COMMUNITY SCHOOL, MILTON KEYNES

As a school, we aim to stage a minimum of two productions each year. These usually fall into the pattern of one drama and one musical. Last year the drama was Macbeth, staged in the professional theatre which forms part of our campus. For the summer musical I decided to stage a production of the ecological musical Yanamamo.

I had staged Yanamamo some six years earlier at a previous school in Bedfordshire, and had fond memories of it as a piece with good music and strong songs, scope for imaginative settings, the involvement of young dancers and gymnasts and large numbers of students in a choir and as accompanying musicians - in short, the ideal school production vehicle.

I originally thought of doing the show simply as 'the school production', but after discussions with our head of music we decided to expand the scope to include one or two local middle schools. That was soon enlarged to include all our contributor middle schools and one or two others as well. Our theatre was beginning to look a bit cramped; if they all came, we would be looking at a choir of two hundred or so. We started to make contingency plans to move into one of the sports halls which would offer more accommodation.

Scores were bought, performance rights applied for, the World Wide Fund for Nature, the publishers and composers invited, along with other national and local nobs. I began designing the set which included a waterfall and stream and half a garden centre of tropical-looking plants to replicate the Amazonian rain forest. Our smoke machine had disappeared or was bust, I can't remember, so we rented a couple.

Joy, and disaster! All the middle schools wanted to take part. The Theatre wasn't going to be big enough. Come to that, the giant sports hall was beginning to look rather anaemic and, anyway, it had rotten acoustics. Word had got around. Local (and rival) upper schools wanted to get involved. We began to look at possible alternative venues. The bill for producing thousands of copies of song lyrics was getting out of hand. The office staff were complaining (quite justly) that they had other things to do.

We decided that as the show was going to take place in the summer term, an outdoor venue might be the answer. The Head's garden was too small (just), so we entered into negotiation with the National Hockey Stadium. The Milton Keynes Youth Orchestra joined in. A rock section was added. Sound and lighting were getting complicated. Someone knew an expert in Holland who was flying in to assist. The Head of Music knew a tropical plant expert who was going to build a jungle. Another choir joined.

Funnily enough, no-one was panicking that, like Topsy, this thing was growing and growing. If it went well, it was going to be the greatest show ever to hit Milton Keynes or the South East Midlands come to that. If it turned out to be a disaster ... Passports were checked!

The Hockey Stadium pulled out. Heads were scratched – no, not Dave McCluskey, our chief. We were by now in the region of

1000 singers and dancers with who knows how many musicians on top of that. We finally found a place big enough to stage our 'school play' in the Bletchley Leisure Centre which we booked for four nights at £700 per night. I was by now fully booked up with the drama exams and the head of music had taken control.

Rehearsals began. A thousand and one things were going on in the background as well as up front. Who says teachers (and parents) are not fully supportive of their schools and communities? We applied for a grant - and didn't get it. A bloke was hired to video the show. The authors and publishers decided to come, so did the World Wide Fund for Nature, so did the Italian Vice Consul. We changed the Rich Tea to Chocolate Digestives.

By the end of it, something like twenty three schools had students participating, including some from neighbouring counties. It took ten minutes just for the choir to file on or off. They were kept under control by one of our teachers who is a singer and fierce, and who had opted to direct the choir.

In the end, it all went pretty smoothly and the band played a treat. I'm currently planning next year's play - Educating Rita - which has just two parts! The head of music tells me he's going to do the follow up to Yanamamo — Ocean Worlds. The North Sea has been booked and dolphins are on order along with the valium.

I've applied for a quieter job as head of tourism in Iraq.

Kevin McKenna

Head of Performing Arts, Sir Frank Markham Community School, Milton Keynes.

RE-LAUNCHING DRAMA IN A COMPREHENSIVE

SIR GRAHAM BALFOUR SCHOOL, STAFFORD

11-16 MIXED COMPREHENSIVE : 650 STUDENTS

Background

Historically the school had had a strong tradition of music and drama, particularly in the 70s and 80s, when the school had a roll of near 1300. In the 1980s Drama was offered as a discrete GCSE subject and several highly successful productions were staged. Unfortunately when rolls fell sharply, Drama was an early casualty, and was incorporated into the English curriculum. Inevitably this led to a much lower profile for the subject, and drama was not used as a means of developing personal feelings and expression.

1995 – 1997

In September 1995 a new Headteacher was appointed who strongly supported Expressive Arts. A fundamental review of the curriculum was undertaken by staff and governors during 1995 - 6 and an Expressive Arts Faculty was formed covering Art, Music, Dance and Drama. The timetabling consisted of one 50 minute lesson each of Drama, Music and Art in Years 8 and 9, and a rotation of all four subjects during a 3 period allocation in Year 7. The existing Head of Technology, who had considerable involvement in local amateur dramatics, took on the leadership of the new faculty. Drama was led on a temporary basis by a modern languages teacher, and dance taught by a female PE specialist.

The Drama course was based largely on the Chalk Face material, with lessons taking place in school halls, corridors and general classrooms. After the first year it became apparent that there was insufficient time in Year 7 for Music, Drama and Art. From September 1997 dance was dropped as a separate lesson and integrated as an extension of Drama.

In September 1997 a specialist Head of Drama (also second in English) was appointed. This enabled us to considerably expand activities and develop extensive links with outside companies and agencies. A drama studio was created by removing a wall between two English rooms, so providing a base for the subject.

September 1997 to date

Since the appointment of the Head of Drama the Department has endeavoured to build upon the good practice previously established, involving pupils in a diverse range of drama activities. These have included the following:

- ZIP Theatre Company production about adolescence and sexuality — Year 10.

- Visit to Shakespeare's "Macbeth", Cannock — Year 11.

- Visit to J.B. Priestley's "An Inspector Calls", Burslem College — Year 11.

- Activity days incorporating Music, Dance and Drama — All Years.

- Performance by Hungarian Dance Company — Year 9.

- Dance Workshop, Stoke — Year 10 English, drama.

The teaching of drama at KS3 has been greatly enhanced by the appointment of a NQT whose determination and imagination in her first year of teaching have brought a fresh perspective and new enthusiasm. Another positive development has been the use made of the drama studio by other subject teachers including foreign languages, history and careers. It was also the venue for the prospective Year 7 parents' evening and will host the Year 7 summer music concert.

The launch of GCSE drama in September 1997 has raised the profile of the subject throughout the school. The fifteen students are extremely hard working and dedicated and have made a flying start to their course by participating in:

- Workshop and production of "Macbeth" with Bitesize Theatre Company;

- Workshop and production "Exposure" by Twisted Stocking Theatre Company, Stafford Gatehouse;

- Performances at all primary contributor schools as part of induction process;

- Running workshops at Year 6 Open Evening;

- An interpretation of "The 12 Days of Christmas" at annual concert and assemblies
  (humorous and highly original);

- Performance, "Task" to Year 9 as part of options process.

Year 7 students participated in a workshop about "The Greeks" in January; the intention is to follow this up once the weather improves with some Greek drama in the school's very own purpose built amphitheatre! The autumn term was spent looking at scripts about moving up to High School, in order to give these new arrivals the chance to air and explore any problems they had encountered.

The students in Year 8 have gone wild enacting cowboys, native American Indians and the 'Wild West' in general. A local expert and parent spoke to the students and bought in artefacts.

In Year 9 the students produced some stunning interpretations of Mussorgsky's "Pictures at an Exhibition". Considering that they had only experienced one year of Drama the standard of mime, inprovisation, concentration and co-operation was outstanding. In the Spring Term Drama supports the preparation for SATs in the English faculty with special approaches to Shakespeare and another visit with workshop from "Bitesize".

The Way Forward

GCSE Drama having been successfully launched, the heads of Drama, Music and Art are now exploring the possibility of introducing GCSE Expressive Arts from September 1998, and GNVQ and A level Performing Arts from September 1999.

The school newsletter, "Balfour News" is regularly inundated with articles about drama in order to maintain its high profile. The benefits of Drama and its techniques as a means to underpin the rest of the curriculum are gradually becoming apparent to the rest of the school. We plan to publish general information about teaching strategies used in Drama lessons, such as rôle play, hot seating and improvisation. These can then be used by other staff in their own subject areas and particularly in PSE.

The successes of the Drama department, including the production of "Oliver!" in April 1998 could not have occurred without the support from all staff, and the commitment of governors, senior staff and parents.

Stephanie Ewan
Head of Drama

THE AESTHETICS FEDERATION

WADDESDON C. OF E. SCHOOL, NR AYLESBURY, BUCKS

A former head extolled the virtues of PE to me by saying that "it pumped the life blood round the system". I think the same may apply to Art, Drama, Music and outdoor pursuits. Despite all the developments of the last 25 years, I believe that schools must still supplement the academic curriculum with a rich variety of creative, sporting and residential experiences.

I was appointed as Head of Waddesdon after an HMI inspection. The management of the curriculum was one of the aspects highlighted as in need of attention. I took the opportunity to create groups of subjects called federations, for two main reasons. I believed that subjects are the best vehicles for teaching the curriculum and I wanted to imply that these were loose groupings liable to reconstitution in the future as the needs of the school changed. In charge of each federation was a curriculum co-ordinator, a title stolen from the primary sector.

As well as the old favourites Mathematics, Science, Humanities and Technology I created federations of Communications and Aesthetics. The latter grouped Art, Drama, Dance and PE. After internal interviews, the Drama teacher was appointed curriculum co-ordinator. I vividly remember a heated conversation with the Head of Science who demanded to know why Drama was now equal with Science in the management hierarchy. That's the problem when you start appointing young upstarts to headship! (He didn't say that, but clearly meant it.)

The appointment of this curriculum co-ordinator was vital and the school was blessed with an outstanding teacher in terms both of classroom teaching and vision. Things have not all been plain sailing, however. Even though Aesthetics is clearly successful, colleagues continue to question the disruption that Art, Music or drama can bring to the daily life of the school. Quite right too - we must not lose sight of the ball! But if we can't cope with a bit of chaos and disruption from time to time, we're not as good as we like to think.

There is a continuing debate about the heavy load of ten GCSEs including compulsory art, music or drama. My view is that it keeps the students focused, has the support of parents, staff and students and gives Aesthetics a special place in our curriculum. Aesthetics provides enrichment and enjoyment for our students and offers more pathways for success.

As to Drama, in particular, I think we should bear in mind that most secondary students can recall vividly performances of live theatre they saw whilst at primary school. The images are still clear and any message often retained quite clearly. How can we build upon this experience and take it forward?

Early in KS3 the emphasis is on group work in class, designed to build confidence, with little focus on performance within lessons. This is followed by the gradual introduction of the skills needed to discuss and evaluate work positively. The students also learn the skills needed to appreciate and analyse live performances. KS3 students sometimes act as the invited audience for GCSE and A level performances. Once you understand how to observe, you may gain the confidence to perform .... in life, that is, not on the stage.

Each term the school holds a performance showcase, giving an opportunity to sing, dance, play or act. The sixth form audition the acts. Competition to perform is fierce, and we always sell out of tickets within hours. It is a chance for the school - students, parents, guests, staff – to celebrate achievement. Once each year an evening of dance is held. In the last few years I have noticed a new phenomenon here .... boys! Where has this confidence come from? Whole school assemblies are still a part of our life at Waddesdon, many organised and conducted by students of all ages. It's part of the culture.

The chaos occurs when we invite African drummers to perform (not very good at just using a 50 minute lesson lasting from 9.10 to 10.00 precisely!); or ask opera companies to hold half day workshops, or arrange dance workshops; or send students to expressive arts workshops – or a whole year group to the theatre; or bring a theatre company into school. All of this is disruptive, and must be handled carefully, but has borne fruit for us.

It is not easy to give an objective critique of the success of the Aesthetics federation venture, as it is part of the overall management strategy and not the central theme. In contemporary terms the school is characterised as succeeding. In February 1998 it was cited in the preface of HMCI's annual report and the DfEE identified its sustained improvement at GCSE as being in the top twenty nationally. At present 59% of students achieve 5 or more A* - C grades at GCSE. Waddesdon values academic achievement, but not exclusively.

Alan Armstrong

Headteacher

EDINBURGH EXPERIENCES

WEY VALLEY SCHOOL, WEYMOUTH

It all started in the dim and distant early nineties. Having co-written two full-length large cast productions for Year 9 pupils, David James - (Disney's Teacher of the Year for the South West region 1997) and Julian Richards agreed that they should look into the idea of taking the first of these productions, "Still Waters" with its full cast of nearly 50, now Year 10 pupils, to the Mecca of all Arts festivals... The "Fringe".

Each Year 9 production takes elements of Key Stage 3 History, combined with English and Drama to bring the past to life in a way that classroom situations cannot. Along the way other subjects joined the throng. Technology and Art played a large part. One particularly talented Art teacher constructed multi-purpose staging that has served all the productions and looks set to continue for a good few more - fingers crossed.

Each of the productions has used different staging, and so far the standard proscenium setting has been forsaken for more experimental modes of performance. (As you can imagine, with the typical sea-side end of the pier type theatre. Weymouth offers the best of theatrical experiences, from summer shows to full-blown Pantomine. Apart from occasions at the Tertiary College, Chichester is the closest theatrical experience that could be out of the norm).

The most important promise for the casting has been our policy of open-access. No auditions are held and casting does not necessarily centre on the academic ability of a child or their previous performance experience. After all, if we always preach to the converted, from whence comes the congregation? We have had leading roles played by students with special needs and - in the words of Laurel & Hardy - no one has been any the wiser. This has confirmed and reinforced this policy, and has shown some pupils in a better light to peers, teachers and parents alike.

The family feeling generated by being in such a production is unbelievable. The students who performed at the "Fringe" that first time (1994) even though some are at University and others working around the country, are still in contact with each other. One member of the cast was unable to enter a college in Bristol to do a

B. Tec course - her GCSE results were not as she had hoped. Performing at the "Fringe" swung it for her and she was accepted on the strength of this experience.

The first trip which tried to keep the open access policy strictly open was a financial nightmare. The promise was to charge £35 per child for the week and the rest to be raised in sponsorship. (Subsequent years have not been run in this way; as we all know sponsorship is harder and harder to obtain as belts are drawn ever tighter in the commercial sector). Were it not for the extremes that David was prepared to go to in securing the funds, and also the support from his long suffering wife, the venture would have foundered. The resultant situation would have been our long expected Titanic impression - icebergs sometimes show 90% above the surface!

As things stood, on a wing and a prayer we took our first steps of pilgrimage to find the great gods of administration were there to trip our jaunty step. The licences for performance were not in place and the fire inspectors were unhappy with certain aspects of our venue, but eventually the curtain went up to an enraptured audience of approximately six people. We had known that this was the average audience at the "Fringe", so we were flying high on our first day.

'Why go through all this?' you may ask. How often do 50-odd fifteen year olds get the chance to sample 3000 paying shows; street entertainment at a fraction of the price; or indeed get the chance to process down the Royal Mile singing in costume whilst leafleting the crowds?

Three trips, 6 original shows, over 150 young people, we were happy with our achievements. Until suddenly, the mobile phone rang. Here was the ultimate privilege; two performances in 1997, by invitation, to the showcase "Pick of the Fringe" stage in Princes Street Park sponsored by Edinburgh's Evening News.

Still the only single 11-16 comprehensive school to ply our wares in this manner, in 1997 our horizons were further broadened. The Wey Valley Theatre Co. were invited to play the Kapolcs Cultural Festival in Budapest. Unfortunately, costs beat us that year but we will be heading for foreign climes in 1999. Meanwhile Edinburgh remains on hold. Perhaps 1999, or even a Millennium visit ... but until then ... Budapest here we come.

Julian Richards

Teacher of Drama

THE YEAR 9 PRODUCTION

THE GRAMMAR SCHOOL FOR GIRLS, WILMINGTON, KENT

There is nothing more motivating to the majority of students than being associated, in whatever capacity, with a stage production. Given this challenge, minor illnesses disappear, absenteeism becomes non-existent, problems with transport at the end of the day turn out not to be problems, students claiming to have little memory recall find they can memorise major parts, moves and all, and others find powers of creativity, originality and business acumen that they never knew they had. Their biggest fear is to be asked to leave the production; their biggest reward is the applause and congratulation they receive and well deserve.

With this in mind, with option choices made and, more recently, SATs over, we introduced, some six years ago, the Year 9 Project.

In effect, this means that the whole of Year 9 is challenged to produce and present, with staff guidance, a complete full-length musical from start to finish in about ten days – sometimes less. We choose musicals because they involve more students in actual performance than plays do, but, since almost all of them want to be 'in it', students are told that the show can't go on unless thirty of them are altruistic enough to choose not to perform (because someone has to shift the scenery, show people to their seats and switch on the urn) – leaving up to ninety of them on stage on the night. Altruism is the first lesson.

The only things that are arranged in advance are the performing rights of the show chosen, and the various groupings. This is done so that, obviously, we know that we have permission to perform whatever it is, and so that appropriate timetabling can be done.

After the SATs we call the whole year group together and tell them what the challenge is to be - what the show is and how long they have to do it. At this stage, they are usually very excited, but rather daunted as well. We also ask them to choose two out of several possible activities - for example, performing, playing, stage crew, set design and painting, properties, costumes, lighting, business management, sales, publicity, front-of-house, refreshments, research and display - there's something for everyone, and an opportunity to try something they haven't done before. All those who wish to audition for a solo part are also asked to indicate this and auditions are held during the following dinner hours.

During the actual days of production, usually the last two weeks of the summer term when Years 11 and 13 have left school, students and appropriate volunteer (and possibly slightly insane) staff are released from timetable, and work begins. As far as possible, students are encouraged to use their own ideas and initiatives, working in self-selected groups, although the shortness of time does necessitate some direction - to make sure, say, that the vast chorus knows what it's doing, or that the Chairman of Governors isn't left off the invitation list.

The students quickly find out that there is much more to a show than being in the limelight, as they buy, cut and sew fabric, persuade local firms to take advertising space in their computer designed programme, send invoices and invitations, keep the finances on an even keel and properly accounted for, work out how to design and make a grand piano or a flying saucer, or calculate how many tea bags are needed for 350 cups of tea. As well as working in school, groups of girls also visit the local civic theatre in Dartford to learn from professional business and front-of-house managers, and stage and lighting crews. If possible, we also take them to a professional evening performance - perhaps in the West End.

The days are run very tightly - students need to be exactly where they are supposed to be at the time they are supposed to be there, taking direction not from a teacher, but from a list on a notice board - and they always are.

We started these productions with "Salad Days", and have now added "My Fair Lady", "Calamity Jane", "Viva Mexico!" and "Follow That Girl". This year's production hasn't been decided yet - the annual school show is still in rehearsal – but there will be one!

At the end of the two evening performances, and the afternoon performance for senior citizens, and after the inevitable clearing up, we ask the students to complete a formal evaluation of the project. What have they learned? Apart from the obvious practical skills they've learned to work as a team, to solve problems, to meet deadlines. They've learned something about each other - very often students reveal incredible talents and qualities previously unsuspected. They've made new friends in forms other than their own and learned to value what others have to offer. They've learned what it's like to be more tired than they've ever been in their lives before - and how to work through it, because the show must go on. They've increased their feelings of belonging, of involvement and of self-esteem. And they've had great fun.

Was it worth it? You bet it was.

What advice would they give us for next year? Do another one!

And what does the rest of the school do while Year 9 is so intensively busy? Well, there's the Year 7 Project and the Year 8 Project and the Year 10 Project – but that's another story ...

Dr Janet Viggers

Head Teacher

DRAMA IN A RURAL BOARDING GM SCHOOL

WYMONDHAM COLLEGE, NORFOLK

Curriculum

Pupils in KS3 have 6 lessons of English per week, representing 13.6% of curriculum time, and departmental schemes of work devote one of these lessons each week to drama which is timetabled where possible in one of two studios with some lighting and sound equipment and blackout facilities - but located in Second World War Nissen huts.

Drama is offered as one of four subjects in the Expressive and Performing Arts block, which enables it to attract just over fifty percent of the students at KS4.

Theatre Studies A level has groups of a dozen or more each year, even though the department also runs A levels in English Literature, English Language and Communication Studies.

Extra-curricular

There has been a major production by the English department every two years – "Grease" in 1997, "A Midsummer Night's Dream" in 1995 and "Nicholas Nickleby" in 1993. For such events – the cast, stage crew and musicians numbered 200 students for "Grease" – the Sports Hall is converted into a theatre with a stage made from industrial scaffolding and the hiring of a bank of 400 tiered seats.

Theatre Studies students stage performances in the larger studio – "A Doll's House" in 1998, "The Resistible Rise of Arturo Ui" and "Our Country's Good" in 1997 as well as performances they devised themselves – and these evening performances are open to other students and to parents.

Drama GCSE students stage regular productions in the same way, with "Living with Lady Macbeth" in 1998 plus various student-devised performances, culminating in a Year 11 Drama Evening. One evening performance per year is also given by each year group in KS3, where the fruits of drama in the English curriculum are on show.

A Lower School play – "Slick" – ran for three nights in 1997 produced by a science teacher, and "The Pirates of Penzance" sang to packed houses for four nights with a producer from the geography department.

The National Theatre Spring Tour visited the College in 1998 and students enjoyed a morning of workshop activities and an afternoon performance.

Further Elements

Three students reached the final auditions for the National Youth Theatre in 1997 and ended up in three West End productions as well as helping with administration at the Edinburgh Festival. The College also provided a number of students for the cast of a professional production at the Theatre Royal in Norwich.

Several governors without the natural link of children in the cast attended 'Grease' and were unanimous in their praise for the quality of the production and their appreciation of the staff time that this represented. Such a major production required underwriting with £1,500 of capitation. The Parents Staff association offered a grant towards the cost of equipment and ticket sales did cover costs. As a GM school we are obliged to put VAT on the ticket price but could offset some of this as expenditure which incurred VAT.

Overall View

In 1996 some governors and senior staff took time out to examine the College's current position and to identify seven Critical Success Factors for the College. Theatre and Performing Arts productions involving many students in both minor- and whole-College events was one of these.

As a grant maintained rural comprehensive school with boarders and day pupils the College has no defined catchment area and needs to attract applicants in order to continue to exist. We are outside the LEA primary-secondary transfer system and within five miles of two LEA 11-18 comprehensive schools. The quality and breadth of drama provision provides a valuable showcase for the College as well as giving students valuable experience of public performance in a variety of venues and ensuring high standards of personal confidence and communication skills.

Paul Spencer Ellis
Vice Principal

PART
3

Statistical
Appendices

APPENDIX 1

	LEA	GM	TOTAL
COMPREHENSIVE SCHOOLS			
Mixed	430	83	513
Boys'	11	7	18
Girls'	21	4	25
GRAMMAR SCHOOLS			
Mixed	7	6	13
Boys'	6	11	17
Girls'	8	10	18
SECONDARY MODERN SCHOOLS			
Mixed	10	3	13
Boys'	1		1
Girls'	3	1	4
		TOTAL	622
INDEPENDENT SCHOOLS			
Mixed	31		
Boys'	22		
Girls'	58		
		TOTAL	111
		GRAND TOTAL	733

THE PRINCIPAL RESPONDENTS

Headteachers/Principals	466	
Deputy Headteachers/Vice Principals	126	
Faculty Heads	33	[6]
Heads of English and Drama	14	
Heads of Drama/Teachers I/C Drama	85	[22]
Others	9	[1]
TOTAL	**733**	

Numbers in brackets indicate where Heads and Deputy Heads officially associated themselves with the response by signing jointly.

IS THERE A SEPARATE DRAMA DEPARTMENT IN THE SCHOOL?

	Sample	Yes	Yes, within Faculty or English	No	No, but part of Faculty or English
STATE SCHOOLS					
Mixed	537	52.5	15.5	13.4	18.6
Boys'	35	37.1	2.9	31.4	28.6
Girls'	43	18.6	20.9	18.6	41.9
INDEPENDENT SCHOOLS					
Mixed	31	58.0		22.6	19.4
Boys'	22	59.1		13.6	27.3
Girls'	58	51.7	6.9	13.8	27.6
ALL SCHOOLS					
	726	50.1	13.4	15.0	21.5

HEADS OF DRAMA DEPARTMENT IN THE SCHOOL?

IS THERE A HEAD OF DEPARTMENT?			
	Sample	Yes	No
STATE SCHOOLS			
	613	77.5	22.5
INDEPENDENT SCHOOLS			
	111	74.8	25.2

PROMOTION POINTS AWARDED, WHERE THE INFORMATION WAS GIVEN					
	Sample	Four/Three	Two	One	Half/Nil
STATE SCHOOLS					
	408	15.4	44.1	36.8	3.7
INDEPENDENT SCHOOLS					
	49	14.3	34.7	26.5	24.5

APPENDIX 4

● IS THERE SEPARATE CAPITATION FUNDING FOR DRAMA?

	Sample	Yes	No	No (through Faculty/ English)
STATE SCHOOLS				
Mixed	521	77.5	9.2	13.3
Boys'	34	58.8	26.5	14.7
Girls'	47	59.6	23.4	17
INDEPENDENT SCHOOLS				
Mixed	31	77.4	19.4	3.2
Boys'	22	77.3	13.6	9.1
Girls'	58	67.2	25.9	6.9

STAFFING WHERE DRAMA IS DELIVERED THROUGH THE ENGLISH CURRICULUM

	Sample	% of Schools	Number of Teachers	% of Teachers Qualified
ALL STATE SCHOOLS				
Mixed	539	21.5	625	33
Boys'	36	44.4	75	26.7
Girls'	47	40.4	99	24.2
GRAMMAR SCHOOLS				
	48	50	114	18.4
INDEPENDENT SCHOOLS				
Mixed	31	38.7	52	13.5
Boys'	22	40.9	56	16.1
Girls'	58	30.5	75	24

APPENDIX 6

● **DRAMA STAFF — ARE THEY QUALIFIED AND IS DRAMA THEIR MAIN SUBJECT?**

	Number of Teachers (%)			% Qualified?		% Main Subject?	
	Male	Female	Total	Yes	No	Yes	No
STATE SCHOOLS							
Mixed	353 (32.1)	745 (67.9)	1098	70.5	29.5	56.6	43.4
Boys'	20 (48.8)	21 (51.2)	41	75.6	24.4	43.9	56.1
Girls'	7 (9.1)	70 (90.9)	77	72.7	27.3	57.1	42.9
INDEPENDENT SCHOOLS							
Mixed	27 (57.4)	20 (42.6)	47	61.7	38.3	59.6	40.4
Boys'	14 (63.6)	8 (36.4)	22	54.5	45.5	45.5	54.5
Girls'	12 (14.3)	72 (85.7)	84	78.6	21.4	67.9	32.1
ALL SCHOOLS							
	433 (31.6)	936 (68.4)	1369	70.7	29.3	56.9	43.1

APPENDIX 8

	Sample	Types of accommodation available				Is Drama restricted by a lack of specialist accommodation?	
		Drama Rooms	Class Rooms	Halls	Other	Yes	No
STATE SCHOOLS							
Comprehensive & Secondary Modern	541	73.9	34.6	67.3	15.7	47.1	52.9
Grammar	45	62.2	24.4	80.0	2.2	51.1	48.9
INDEPENDENT SCHOOLS							
	102	61.8	46.2	78.4	35.3	40.2	59.8
ALL BY GENDER							
Mixed	533	73.5	35.5	67.4	16.9	47.5	52.5
Boys'	55	54.5	38.2	78.2	20.0	44.0	60.0
Girls'	100	69.0	41.0	78.0	22.0	44.0	56.0
ALL SCHOOLS							
	688	72.1	36.5	69.8	17.9	46.4	53.6

Sample	Nil/Very Little	Advis-ers	T.I.E.	Theatre Groups	Local Support	Other	Charged For	Free
LOCAL AUTHORITY SCHOOLS								
497	21.3	33	33.2	15.1	12.7	3.2	62.6	28.8
GRANT MAINTAINED SCHOOLS								
125	27.2	19.2	25.6	19.2	25.6	7.2	72.8	8
INDEPENDENT SCHOOLS								
111	43.2	8.1	8.1	26.1	6.3	14.4	46.8	16.2

N.B.

'Local support' includes arts groups, drama associations, networks, personal contacts, theatres.

'Other' includes artists in residence and other specialists, college and university departments, examination board inset

See also Part Four for a list of arts, drama and theatre organisations identified as helpful to schools and colleges in the survey.

APPENDIX 9

APPENDIX 10

	Compulsory Throughout?			How Delivered, When Available		
	In Drama	In English	No	Separate Subject	Arts Circus	In English
STATE SCHOOLS						
Comprehensive & Secondary Modern	60.7	17.5	21.8	60.1	15.4	24.5
Grammar	31.5	48.1	20.4	32.6	8.2	59.2
INDEPENDENT SCHOOLS						
	31.8	24.3	43.9	42.0	19.6	38.4
ALL BY GENDER						
Mixed	59.6	17.8	22.6	58.8	15.8	25.4
Boys'	24.0	33.3	42.7	34.8	18.2	47.0
Girls'	42.3	27.7	30.0	48.8	13.6	37.6
ALL SCHOOLS						
	53.9	20.6	25.5	55.4	15.6	29.0

N.B.

1. When Drama is not compulsory throughout Key Stage 3 its availability is restricted either by not being in the curriculum at all, or only in some year groups or for some pupils.

2. The category Arts Circus also includes other timetabling arrangements involving Combined Studies, Information Technology, Physical or Religious Education.

● DRAMA IN KEY STAGE 4

	Is there a Drama Option?		Is there a Combined Course?		Is some Drama required in KS4?	
	YES	NO	YES	NO	YES	NO
STATE SCHOOLS						
Comprehensive & Secondary Modern	86.4	13.6	12.3	87.7	8.2	91.8
Grammar	50.0	50.0	-	100.0	27.1	72.9
INDEPENDENTS						
	53.2	46.8	2.7	97.3	10.8	89.2
ALL BY GENDER						
Mixed	86.1	13.9	11.5	88.5	8.3	91.7
Boys'	45.8	54.2	1.7	98.3	6.8	93.2
Girls'	59.0	41.0	6.7	93.3	20.0	80.0
ALL SCHOOLS						
	79.0	21.0	10.0	90.0	9.9	90.1

● ARE SCHOOLS AWARE OF GENDER IMBALANCE IN GCSE DRAMA?

	No	Yes	If Yes, where specified More Girls	More Boys
ALL MIXED SCHOOLS				
	56.2	43.8	79.1	7.6

CURRICULUM PROVISION FOR DRAMA POST-16

	Is Drama/Theatre Studies available?			Does availability influence curriculum choice at KS4?		
	Sample	Yes	No	Sample	Yes	No
STATE SCHOOLS						
Comprehensive & Secondary Modern	348	77.0	23.0	263	39.5	60.5
Grammar	47	66.0	34.0	30	33.3	67.7
INDEPENDENT SCHOOLS						
	107	77.6	22.4	67	40.3	59.7
ALL BY GENDER						
Mixed	361	77.3	22.7	276	40.9	59.1
Boys'	54	63.0	37.0	23	34.8	65.2
Girls'	87	79.3	20.7	61	32.8	67.2
ALL SCHOOLS						
	502	76.1	23.9	360	39.2	60.8

● THE WIDER USE OF DRAMA IN OTHER ASPECTS OF
SCHOOL LIFE

	Sample	Role-Play	Personal & Social Education	Assemblies
STATE SCHOOLS				
Comprehensive & Secondary Modern	574	28	64.8	52.1
Grammar	48	29.1	64.6	68.7
INDEPENDENT SCHOOLS				
	111	24.3	51.4	64.9
SCHOOLS BY GENDER				
Mixed	570	28.2	64.7	51.8
Boys'	58	20.7	62	53.4
Girls'	105	27.6	57.1	74.3
ALL SCHOOLS				
	733	26.7	63.4	54.4

● CURRENT TRENDS FOR DRAMA PROVISION

	Sample	Increase	Stable	Decrease
STATE SCHOOLS				
Comprehensive & Secondary Modern	572	50.5	37.4	12.1
Grammar	47	66	25.5	8.5
INDEPENDENT SCHOOLS				
	110	69.1	28.2	2.7
ALL BY GENDER				
Mixed	569	53.4	35.7	10.9
Boys'	56	53.5	30.4	16.1
Girls'	107	57.9	34.6	7.5
ALL SCHOOLS				
	732	54.1	35.1	10.8

PART
4

EXTERNAL SUPPORT
AGENCIES AND
SCHOOL PRODUCTIONS

• DO PARENTS AND GOVERNORS AFFECT DECISIONS ON DRAMA?

	Sample	Parents		Governors	
		Yes	No	Yes	No
STATE SCHOOLS					
Comprehensive & Secondary Modern	530	35.3	64.7	43.7	56.3
Grammar	46	43.5	56.5	47.8	52.2
INDEPENDENTS					
	107	40.7	59.3	32.1	67.9
ALL SCHOOLS					
	683	36.7	63.3	42.2	57.8

• ARE SCHOOL THEATRE PRODUCTIONS IN GOOD HEALTH?

	Sample	Excellent	Yes	Just	No
STATE SCHOOLS					
Comprehensive & Secondary Modern	534	5.2	67.8	10.3	16.7
Grammar	48	6.2	68.8	10.4	14.6
INDEPENDENT SCHOOLS					
	107	6.5	85.0	4.8	3.7
ALL BY GENDER					
Mixed	534	6.0	69.7	9.5	14.8
Boys'	55	9.1	67.3	14.5	9.1
Girls'	100	1.0	77.0	6.0	16.0
ALL SCHOOLS					
	689	5.5	70.5	9.5	14.5

For interest this section shares information about Arts, Drama and Theatre Organisations identified as helpful to schools and colleges in the survey.

Please note:

- The list is by no means exhaustive – apologies to any omitted.
- Many of the organisations listed will only be known in particular local areas, but there will be many similar elsewhere.

ARTS ORGANISATIONS *(Listed Under Geographical Titles)*

- Avon Drama Association
- Cleveland
- Derby
- Leicestershire
- Lewisham
- Northern
- Nottingham
- Sheffield
- South West
- Southern
- Yorkshire & Humberside

THEATRES

- Belgrade, Coventry
- Bristol Old Vic
- Cambridge Arts
- Charles Luger, Sutton
- Crucible, Sheffield
- Derby Playhouse
- Dukes Playhouse, Lancaster
- Everyman, Cheltenham
- Globe
- Greenwich Young People's
- Hull Truck
- Kenneth More, Ilford
- Lyric, Hammersmith
- New Victoria, Newcastle-under-Lyne
- Palace, Watford
- Royal Court
- Royal Exchange, Manchester
- Royal National
- Royal Shakespeare Company
- Royal, Northampton
- Theatre Royal and Playhouse, Nottingham
- Wakefield Opera House
- West Yorkshire Playhouse

GENERAL

- Birmingham Ballet
- Central School
- Central Television
- Goldsmith's College
- Kent Shakespeare Project
- Lowry Project
- National Association of Drama Teachers
- National Independent Schools Drama Association
- Opera North
- Royal Ballet

Choice of production featured as an issue in some schools. For interest this list identifies, from information provided, productions mounted in 1996/97.

Please note:

Titles are listed in alphabetical order – figures indicate numbers of productions if more than one.

The list may not be complete – apologies to any omitted.

Some productions were home-grown, and, as such, their titles may not be recognised by others:

The Absurd Person Singular	
Adrian Mole	2
After Magritte	
Animal Farm	3
Anna Karenina	
Annie	8
Annie Get Your Gun	
Antigone	2
Anything Goes	
As You Like It	2
Asleep under the Dark Earth	
The Bacchae	
The Beggar's Opera	
Big Al	
The Birthday Party	2
Blinded by the Sun	
Blood Brothers	7
Blood Wedding	2
Le Bourgois Gentlehomme	
The Boy Friend	9
Bugsy Malone	17
Burning Everest	
Cabaret	9
Calamity Jane	
Camelot	2
Camino Real	
Candide	

/continued...

/continued...

/continued...